NEOCLASSICISM

Author: Victoria Charles

Layout:
Baseline Co. Ltd,
District 3, Ho Chi Minh City
Vietnam

ISBN: 978-1-68325-928-2

Printed in

Victoria Charles

NEOCLASSICISM

Antiquity reborn in reason, harmony,
and heroic ideals

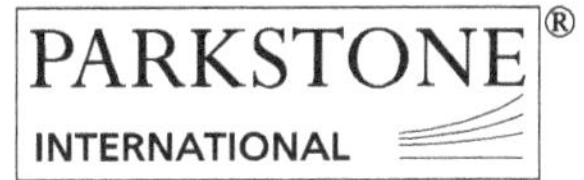

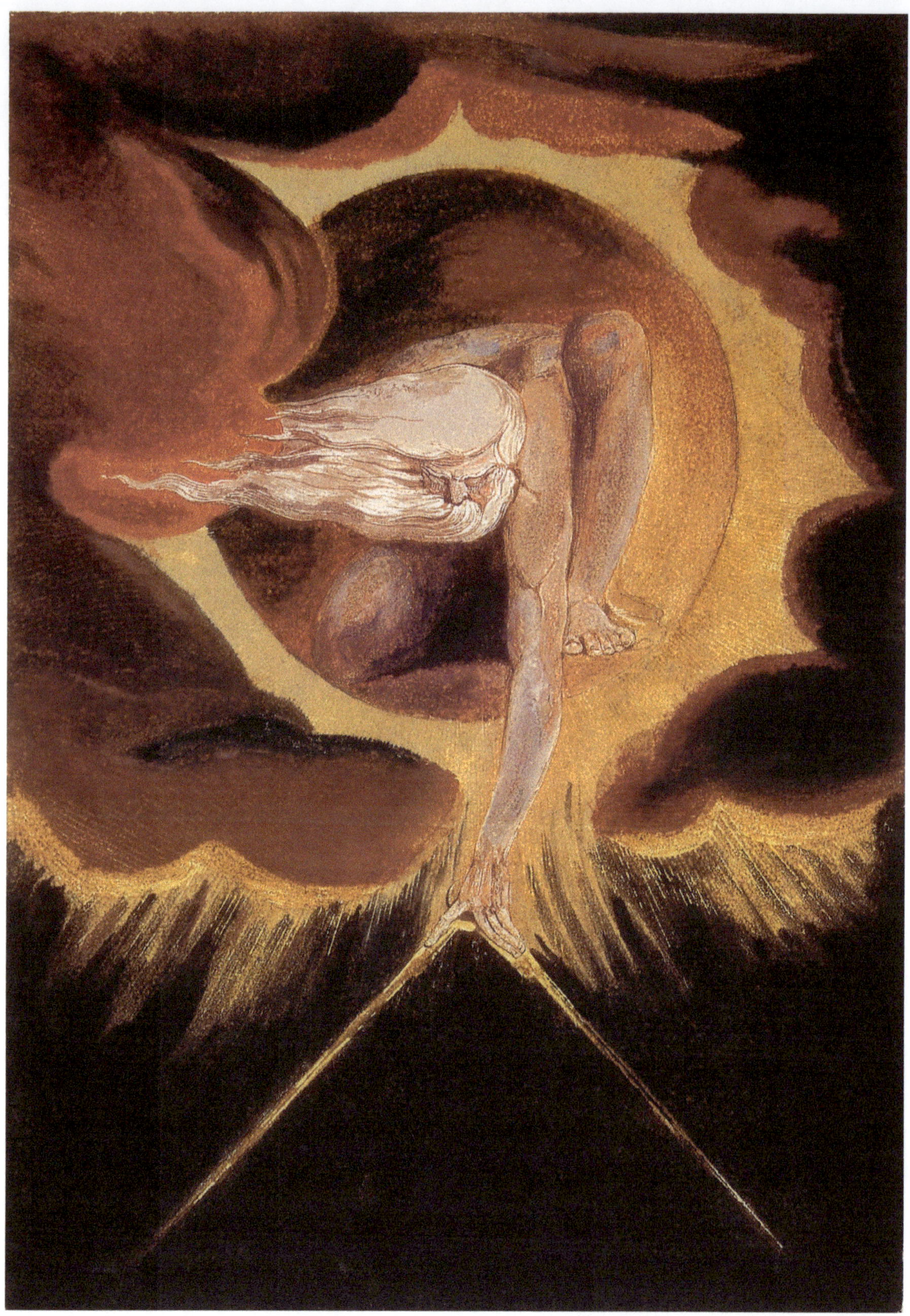

CONTENTS

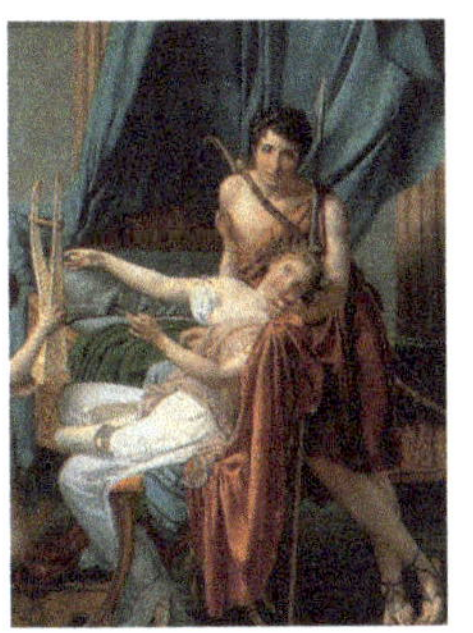

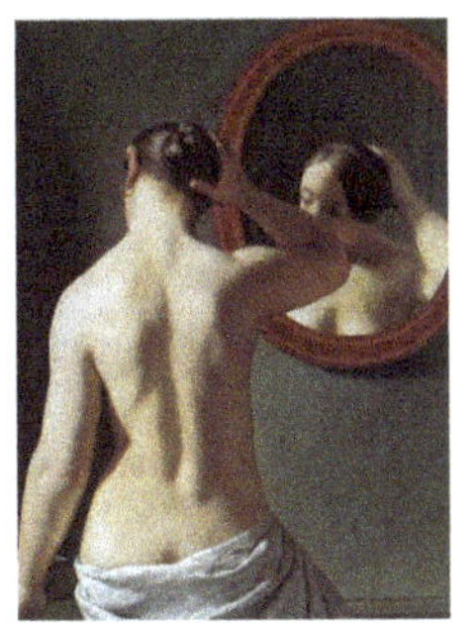

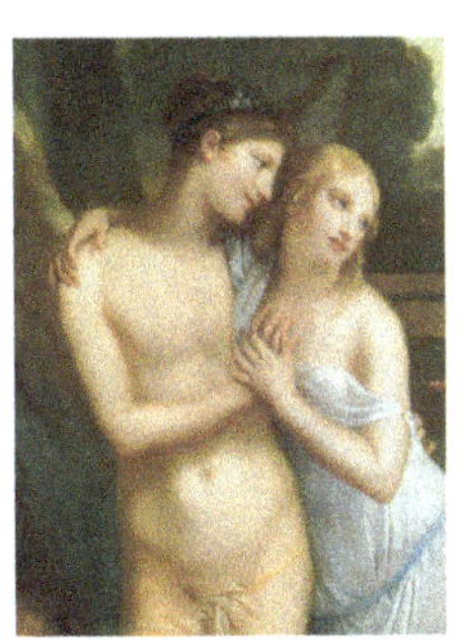

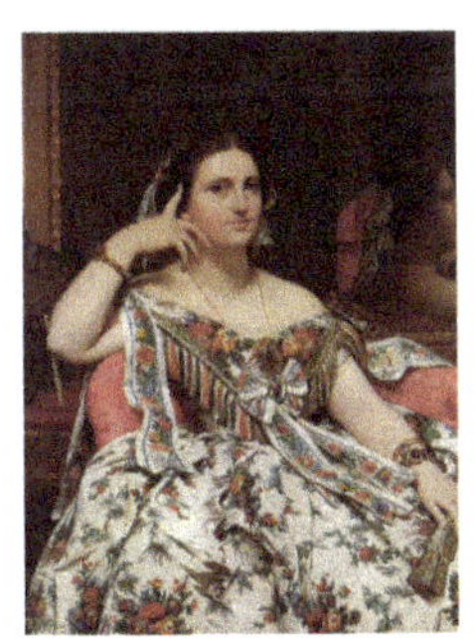

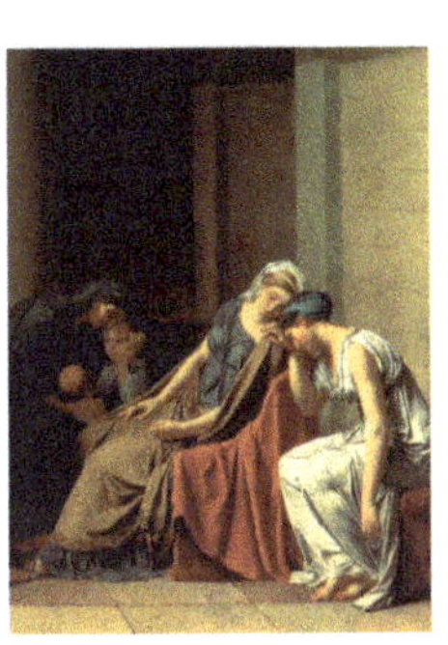

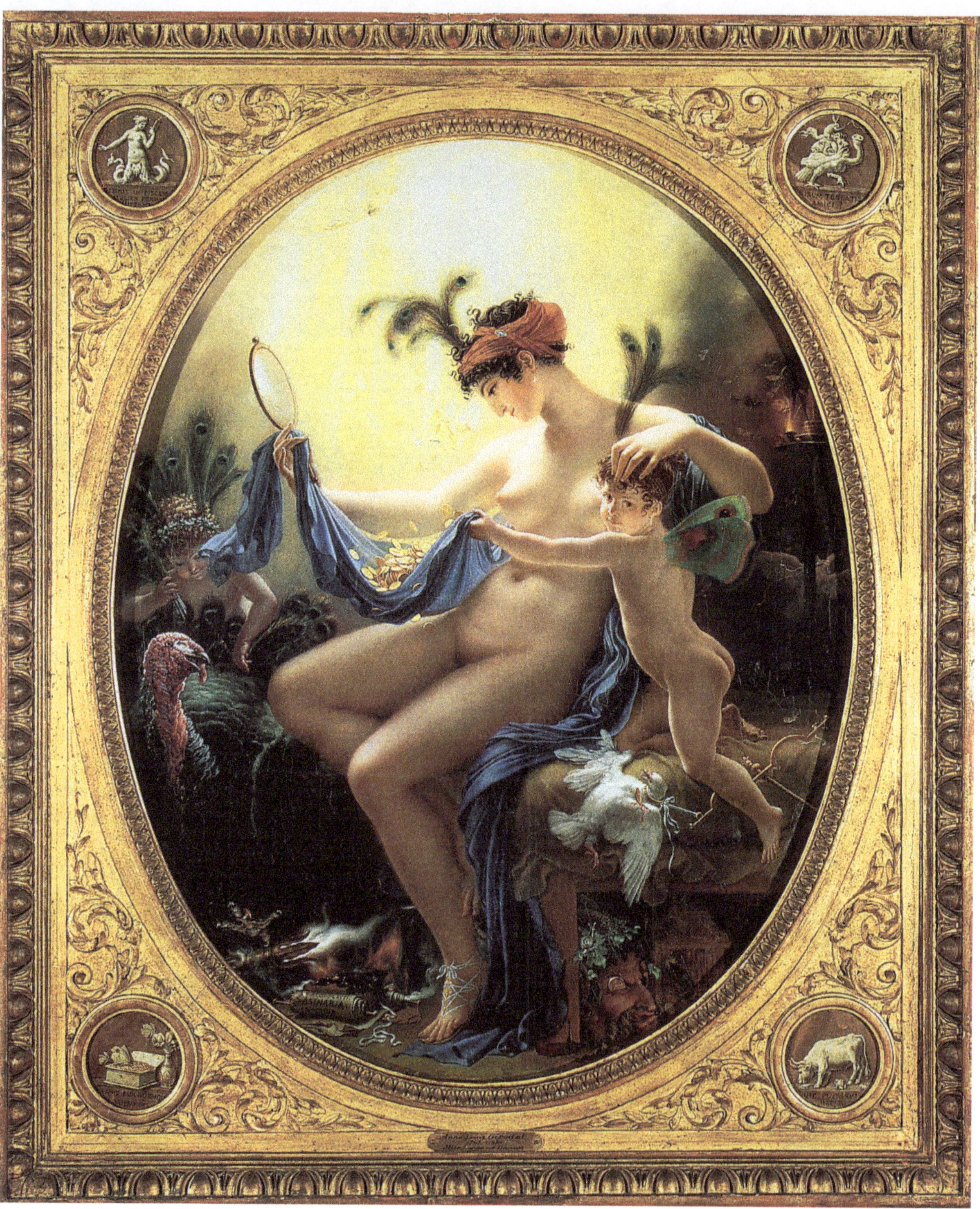

INTRODUCTION

The Enlightenment marks the eighteenth century as a period heavily invested in ideas. Salon culture developed through the taste and social initiative of women during the Rococo period in the courts of France, Austria and Germany. These women were known as *femmes savants,* or learned women. In addition to art, the salons propagated Enlightenment ideas that rejected superstition and favored provable theories based on scientific methods. Empiricism flourished, coming out of the seventeenth century achievements in science, notably those of Britons Sir Isaac Newton (1642 – 1727) and John Locke (1632 – 1727). Their insistence on tangible data and empirical proof changed the course of ideas. In France, the *philosophes* helped to spread rational ideas based on reason into the areas of church and state. They believed that through the progress of ideas, there existed a possibility for the perfection of mankind. Gathering and ordering knowledge was part of the Enlightenment project. Accordingly, Diderot (1713 – 1784) created the first encyclopedia (thirty-five volumes 1751 – 1780) in an attempt to systematically record all existing knowledge. Diderot also became the first art critic by publishing his commentaries on the official French Salon exhibitions of the Royal Academy of Painting and Sculpture. Voltaire (1694 – 1778) wrote against the despotic rule of kings and the hegemony of the church. Later, revolutionary thinkers would recall his seminal ideas. Natural history and zoology were catalogued by the Comte de Buffon (1707 – 1788), while in Sweden Carolus Linnaeus created a comprehensive classification of plants.

Worldwide, the eighteenth century marks the start of the 'modern' period in which a self-conscious awareness of the present in relation to past begets a preoccupation with newness, or being current. Americans in the colonies were also noted for their commitment to Enlightenment ideas, most notably Benjamin Franklin and Thomas Jefferson. Scientific

▲ **William Blake**, 1757-1827, Romanticism, English,
The Ancient of Days, 1794.
Etching in relief with watercolour, 23.3 x 16.8 cm.
The British Museum, London.

◀ **Anne-Louis Girodet,**
1767-1824, Neoclassicism, French,
Mademoiselle Lange as Danaë, 1799.
Oil on canvas, 60.3 x 48.6 cm.
Minneapolis Institue of Arts, Minneapolis.

inventions flourished as much as social inventions, and the Industrial Revolution began in England in the 1740s. It was spurred on by research into steam power, electricity, the discovery of oxygen, and mechanical advances in technology, including the first use of iron for a bridge in 1776.

Born on the eve of the Age of Revolution, Neoclassicism reflected the intellectual, social and political changes of that period. The advent of revolutionary movements in France and America, based on classical ideals such as the democracy of ancient Athens and Rome, made Neoclassical art even more appealing. As three quarters of the French were illiterate, it created an opportunity for art to become a political tool to arouse revolutionary fervor.

The nineteenth century was a century of upheaval, of ferment of new forces and new ideas in conflict with the old. The two great storm centers were France, torn by its Revolution, with its political, social, and economic realignments; and England, disorganized by its Industrial Revolution, with its equally vast social and economic as well as cultural consequences. The freedom of inquiry and liberal thought born of the Renaissance bore fruit luxuriantly in France in the eighteenth century, notably in the work of the Encyclopedists and Rousseau, and voices were already raised in denunciation of social and economic injustice. By the end of the century this expression flared into action in the French Revolution. The Thirteen Colonies in North America had already separated from England, but it was the upheaval in France that caused repercussions throughout both Europe and the Latin American colonies, where French thought and influence had been strong, so that before

the middle of the nineteenth century all the Middle, Central, and South American colonies of Spain and Portugal had severed political connections with their mother countries and set up republics. Europe saw the abolition or the limitation of kings and aristocracy in favor of constitutional monarchies or republics, and the consequent rise of the bourgeoisie and the lower classes into positions previously limited to the aristocracy — with a consequent shaking of traditional culture. The Industrial Revolution, starting in England, where scientific research and applied science ushered in the Machine Age, spread rapidly. The half-century from 1800 to 1850 saw the first of many inventions: steamboat, locomotive, transatlantic liner, and passenger train as well as the telegraph and the camera — all which, with other factors, eventuated in a great expansion of industry; in the rise of the wealthy manufacturer to challenge the wealthy landowner; in the drift of population to the cities where the manufacturing plants were located, with consequent overcrowding; in the emergence of those social and economic conditions which gave rise to socialism and other attempts to alleviate their injustice. The application of the scientific viewpoint, with its critical observation of phenomena, produced Darwin's The Origin of Species (1859) and a consequent long line of research; and a weakening of religious faith.

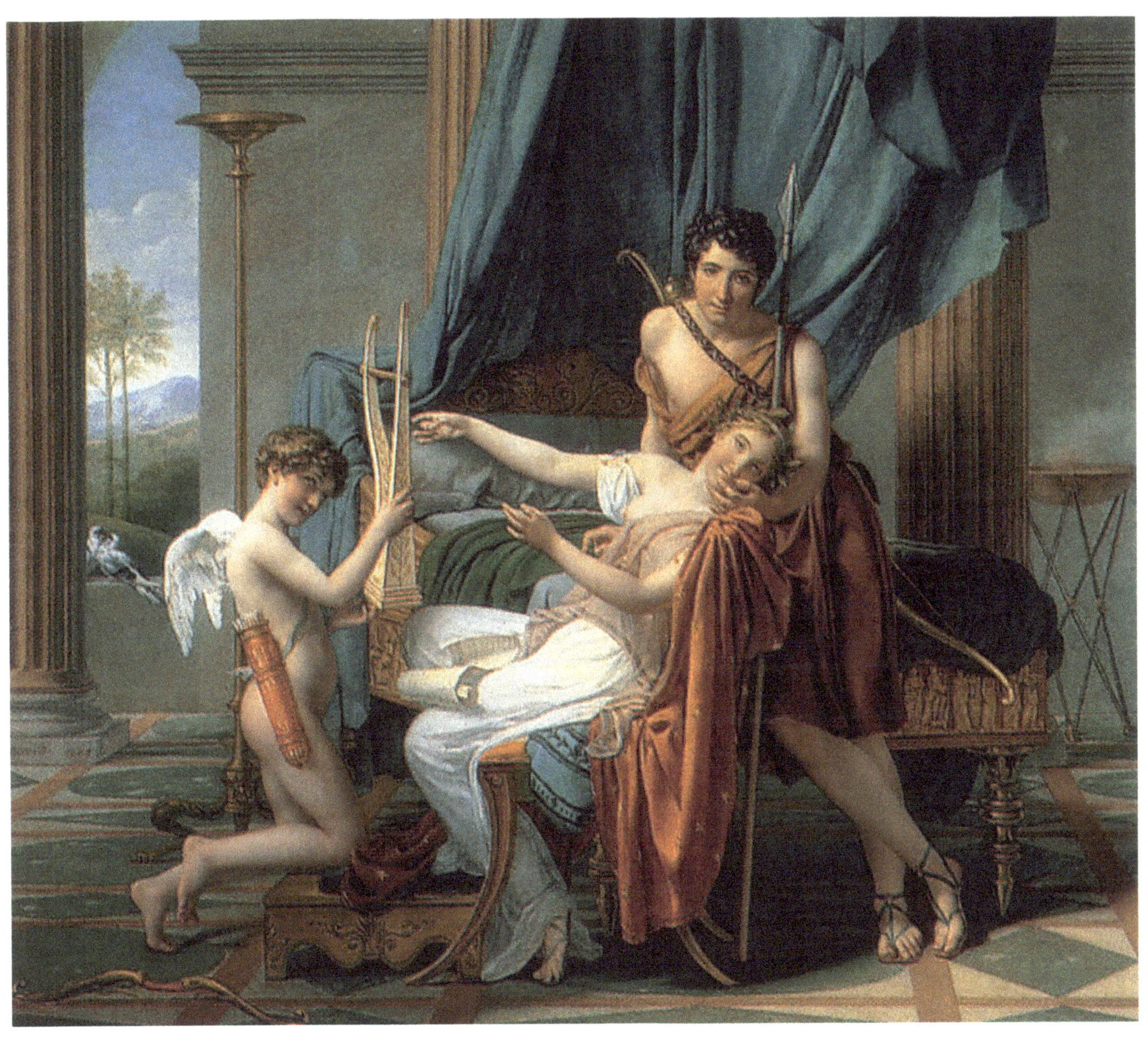

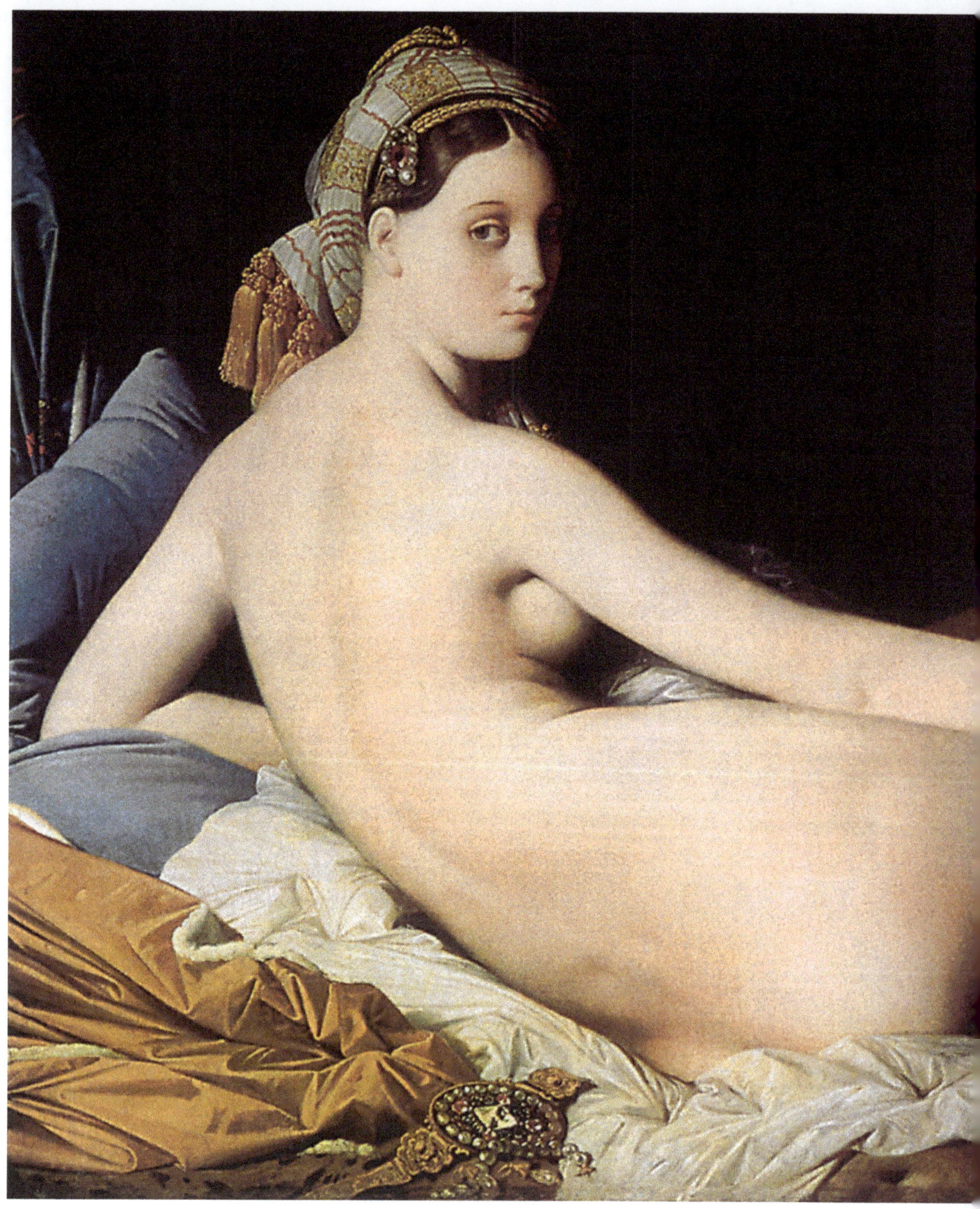

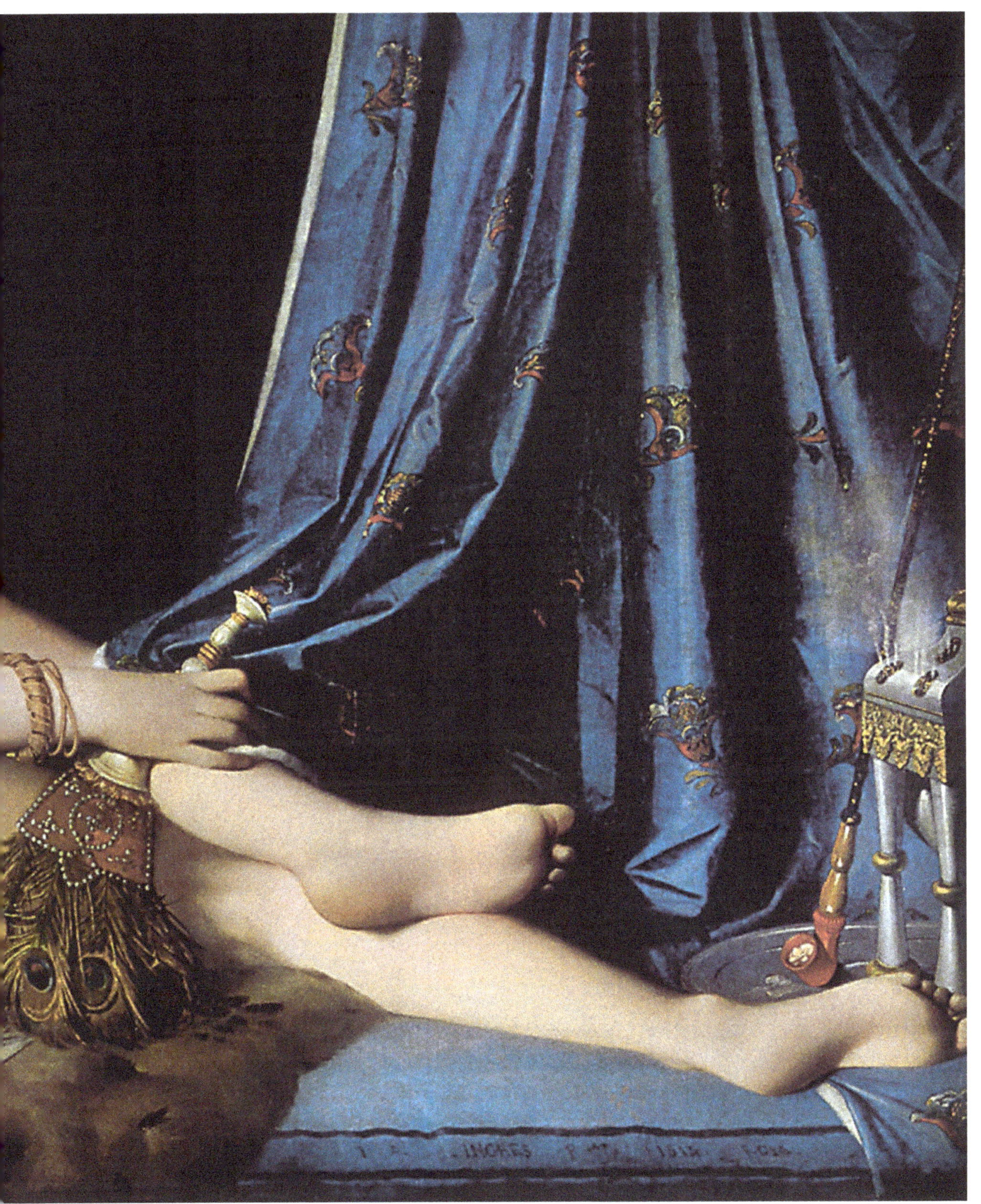

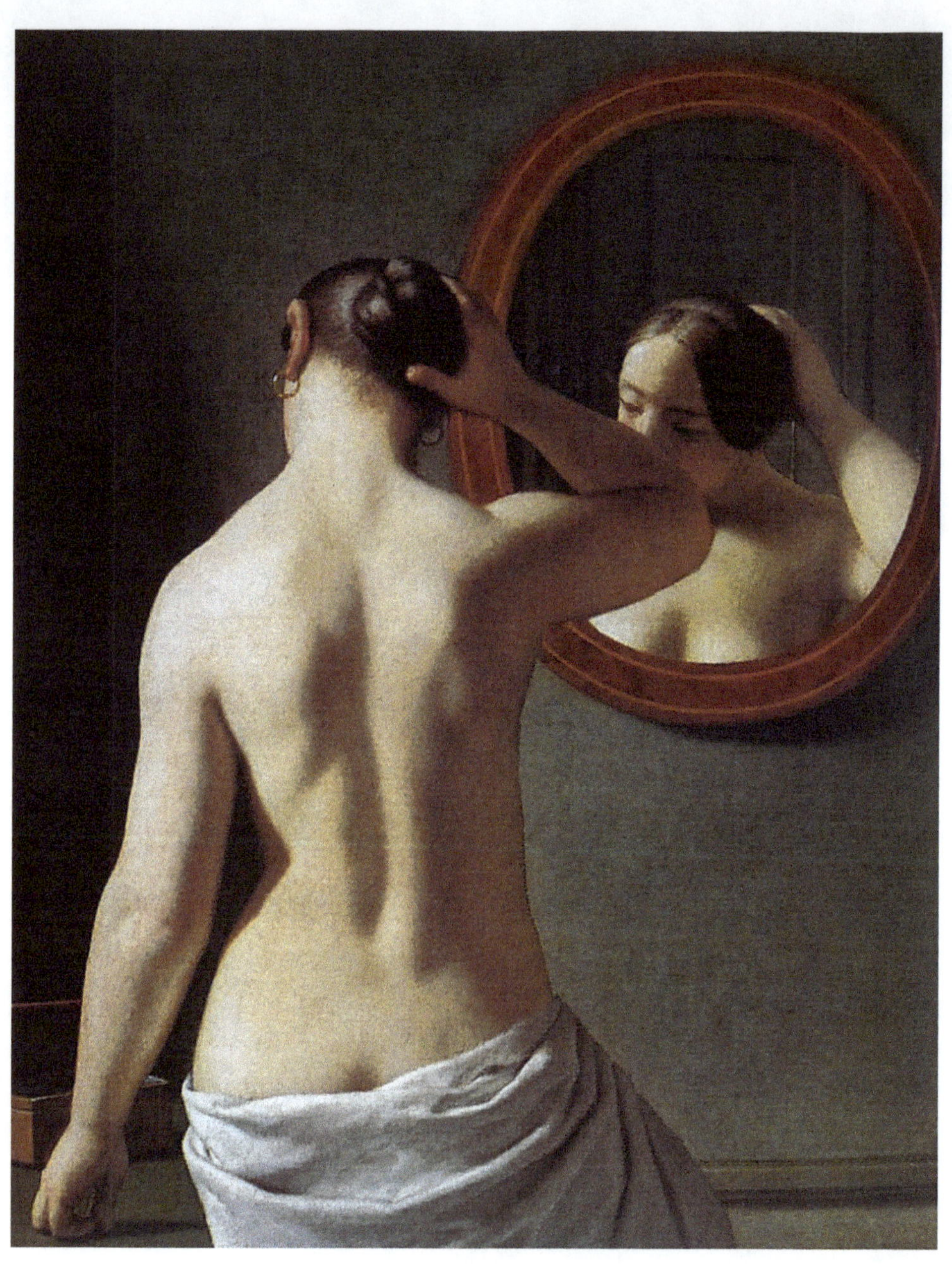

A HISTORY OF NEOCLASSICISM

The Precursors of Neoclassicism

A focus in the eighteenth century on particular social virtues – patriotism, moderation, duty to family, the necessity to embrace reason and study the laws of nature – were at odds with the subject matter and hedonistic style of Rococo painters. Rococo was associated with the decadent 'ancien régime', whose painters were forced to flee the country or change their styles. In the realm of art theory and criticism, the philosophers and writers Diderot and Voltaire were unhappy with the Rococo style flourishing in France, and its days were numbered.

It is, however, to the *Fêtes Champêtres and galantes* of Watteau, Lancret, and Pater, that we must look for the best painting of the time. Elegant and fashionably dressed ladies and gentlemen dance gracefully amid artificial sylvan scenes upon the canvases of Watteau; but trivial as are his subjects, there is a charming grace and touch of nature

◄ **Christoffer Wilhelm Eckersberg,**
Woman with a Mirror (detail), 1841. Neoclassicism.
Oil on canvas, 33.5 x 26 cm.
Hirschprung Collection, Copenhagen.

about his treatment of them that saves him from vulgarity or triviality, and gives him an enduring position. Lancret and Pater treated similar subjects without the delicate genius of Watteau.

Amid the corrupt society of the regency, no place could be found for religious or historical painting; but an art which reflected the superficial charm, the graceful manners, and the elegant frivolity of that society was from the first sure of success, as it was completely representative of the spirit of the times.

Watteau shows us only the amiable and charming side of society in the eighteenth century, the coarse and vicious side is to be seen on the canvases of Francois Boucher, overlaid, indeed, with a grace and charm worthy of Watteau. The versatile genius of Jean Honoré Fragonard rivaled Watteau in the poetic feeling of some of his *Fêtes galantes*, and in others surpassed Boucher in indecency; his work is the culmination of this graceful style which alone brightens up the decadence of the 18th century.

Two painters, indeed, returned from this artificial society to the truthful representation of real life:

Jean Baptiste Chardin, who for his firm, truthful, unaffected painting, the direct simplicity of his composition, and, above all, the genuine humor which pervades all his work, has been justly called the French Hogarth; and Jean Baptiste Greuze, who is best known among us for the charming but mannered heads of girls that are to be seen in every public or private collection. His fame is as a painter of simple scenes of bourgeois life *The Village Bridegroom* The Father explaining the Bible to his Children, and many others — scenes often full of exaggerated sentiment, frequently showing weaknesses of execution, but always touching and graceful. It is, however, not to these men, but to Jacques Louis David, that the reform of French painting is due. The excavations of Pompeii, which were begun in the middle of the eighteenth century, and the consequent studies of Greek art, the results of which were embodied in Winckelmann's Treatise and Lessing's famous Essay, gave a new impulse to the study of ancient art. When David went as a student at Rome, Canova was already at work there.

The humble naturalism of Jean Baptiste Chardin was based in the Dutch still-life artistry of the previous century, while Anglo-American and English painters such as John Singleton Copley of Boston, Joseph Wright of Derby and Thomas Hogarth painted in styles, which, in different ways, embodied a kind of fundamental naturalism that reflected the spirit of the age. A number of artists, such as Elisabeth Vigée-Lebrun and Thomas Gainsborough, incorporated into their paintings some of the lightness of touch that characterized the Rococo, but they modified its excesses and avoided some of its artificial and superficial qualities, however delightful these are.

Many painters co-existed chronologically with more classical artists, and a certain amount of rivalry existed between them. Some late eighteenth- and early-nineteenth century European painters were explicitly interested in the irrational, such as Henry Fuseli in his work *Nightmare*, and Francisco Goya in some of his violent paintings of death and madness. Théodore Gericault explored insanity in some of his smaller paintings, along with themes of death, cannibalism and political corruption in his massive canvas *Raft of the Medusa*. More subtle were the painters of this period who explored the emotional effects of landscape art. John Constable's flickering light and careful study of clouds and sunlight on trees in the English countryside yielded strikingly emotive results.

The German Caspar David Friedrich, on the other hand, evoked the religious mysticism of the landscape, while the American Hudson River School painters, such as Thomas Cole, represented the warm autumnal colors and desolation of a New World wilderness that was quickly disappearing. J. M. W. Turner's paintings of seascapes, landscapes and historical scenes seemed to his contemporaries to be made of 'tinted steam', and he even edged

Théodore Géricault, ▶
1791-1824, Romanticism, French, *Raft of the Medusa*, c. 1818.
Oil on canvas, 491 x 716 cm.
Musée du Louvre, Paris.

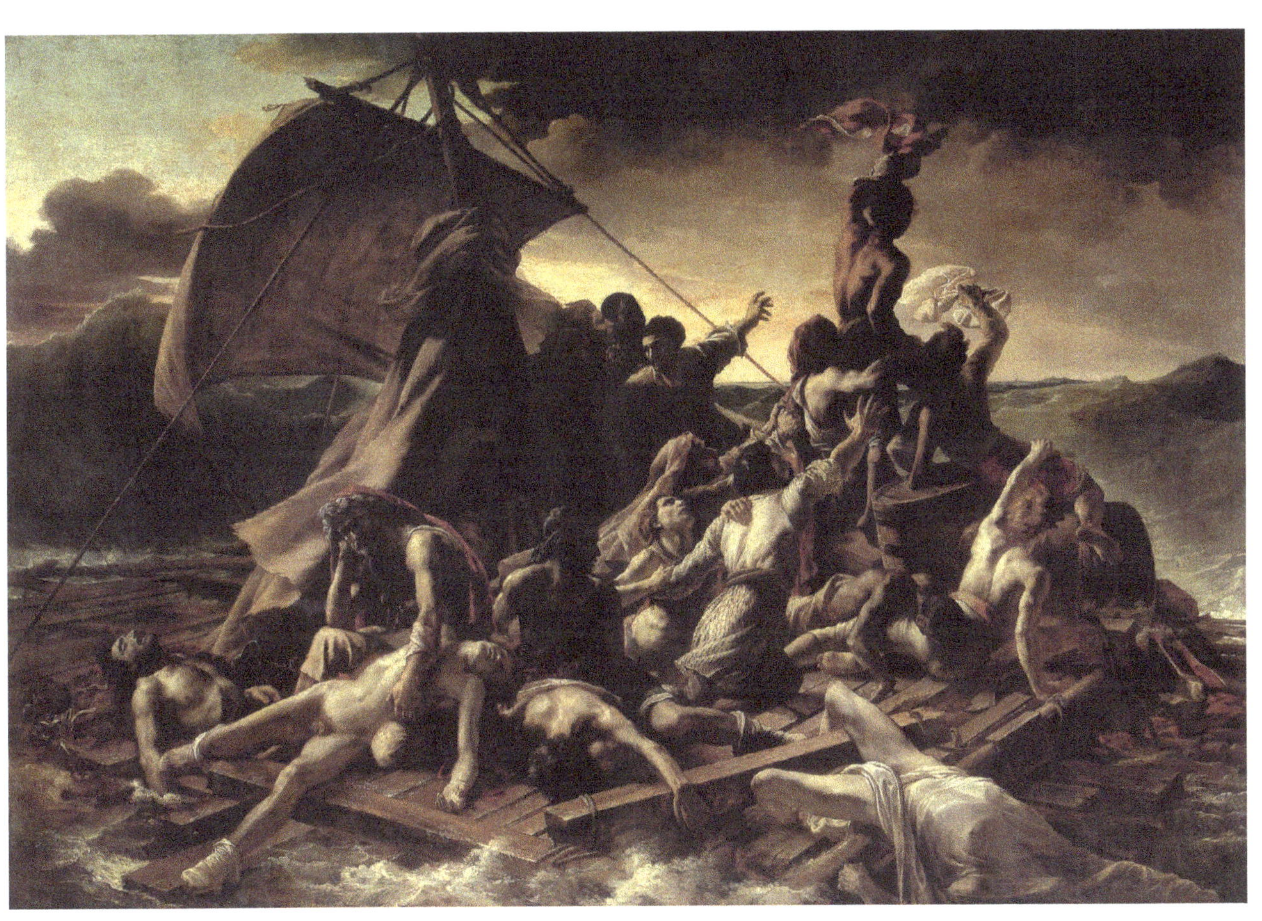

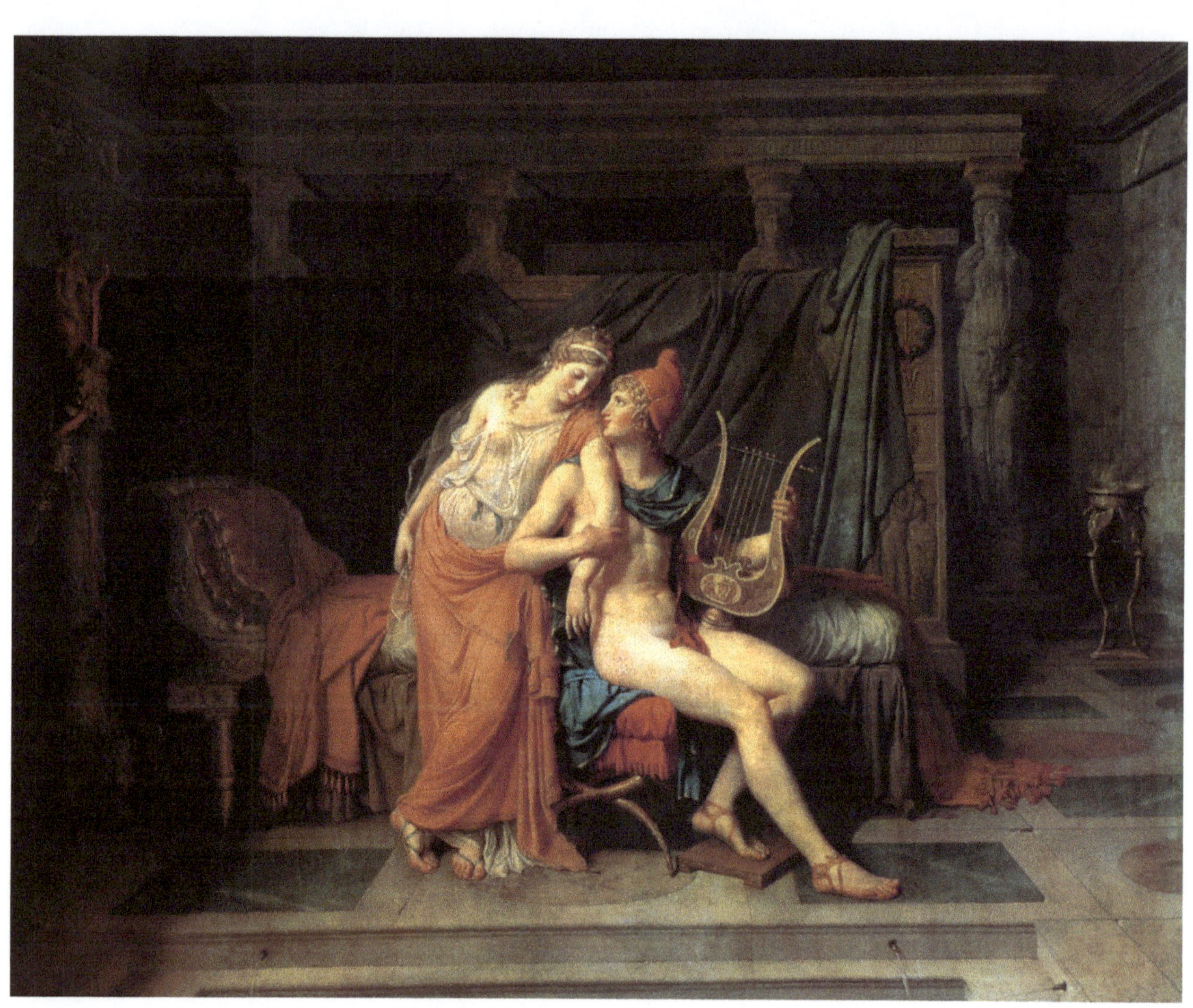

towards modernism in his abstractness. The most influential and acclaimed of the French Romantic painters was Eugène Delacroix. He turned to the High Baroque artist Rubens for artistic inspiration, painting canvas after canvas of tiger hunts, Passion of Christ imagery, and the exotic world of Arab warriors and hunters in northern Africa. Like the Baroque masters before him, Delacroix used dramatic spatial diagonals, cut-off compositional elements and bravura colorism with great effect. Delacroix gained the artistic and even personal enmity of Ingres, prompting contemporaries to recognize in their art the timeless struggle of line versus color.

The influence of David was combined with the love of nature in Jean-Auguste-Dominique Ingres, and the union produced the most perfect work of the French school. He seized, far more deeply than his master, the beauty of ancient statues, and his figures, though classic, are endowed with life and character. His coloring is slight, and wanting in lights and shadows. A beautiful figure, *La Source*, begun in early life, and finished not long before his death, embodies all his best characteristics, and has been called the finest figure in the French school.

Neoclassicism remained in vogue in France through the Napoleonic age, and the elegant linearity style of Jean-Auguste-Dominique

◀ **Jacques-Louis David**,
The Love of Paris and Helen, 1788. Neoclassicism.
Oil on canvas, 146 x 181 cm.
Musée du Louvre, Paris.

Ingres replaced the works of David, who had later softened his approach to create a more decorative form of classicism suitable for the less bourgeois character of the French Empire. If the eighteenth century was the Age of Reason and the Enlightenment, developing at the same time was an intellectual trend towards interest in the irrational and emotional.

The Neoclassical Period

A leitmotif of Western painting has been the persistence of classicism, and here the Rococo found its fiercest opponent. The essentials of the classical style – a dynamic equilibrium, idealized naturalism, measured harmony, restraint of color and a dominance of line, all operating under the guiding influence of ancient Greek and Roman models – reasserted themselves in the late-eighteenth century in response to Rococo. When Jacques-Louis David exhibited his *Oath of the Horatii* in 1785, it electrified the public, and was applauded by the French including the king, gaining an international audience. Thomas Jefferson happened to be in Paris at the time of the painting's exhibition and was greatly impressed.

Neoclassicism is characterized by clarity of form, sober colors, shallow space, strong horizontal and verticals that render that subject matter timeless. The popularity of Neoclassicism preceded the French Revolution, but once the revolution occurred, it became the official style

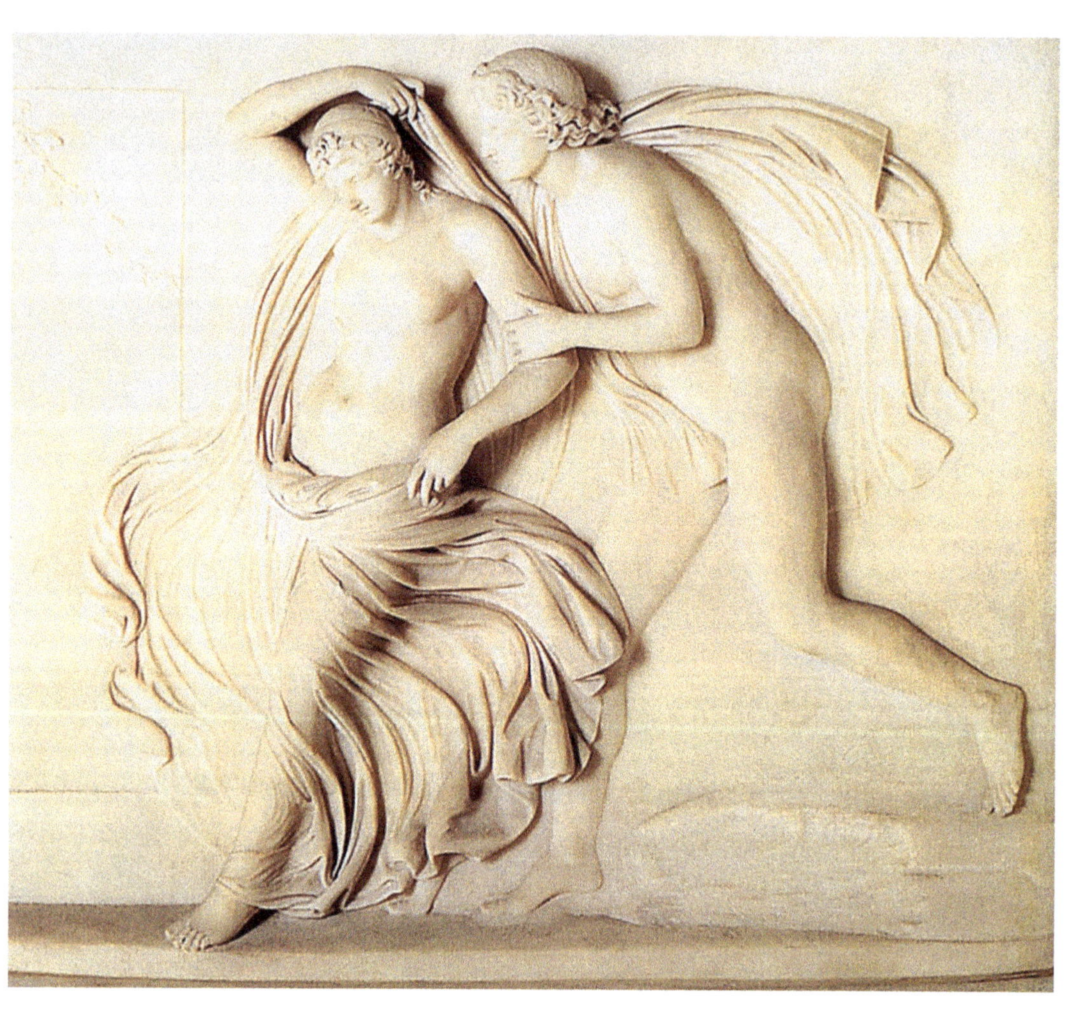

▲ **John Flaxman**,
Apollo and Marpessa, 1790-1794.
Neoclassicism. Marble, 48.4 x 54.8 x 63 cm.
Royal Academy of Arts, London.

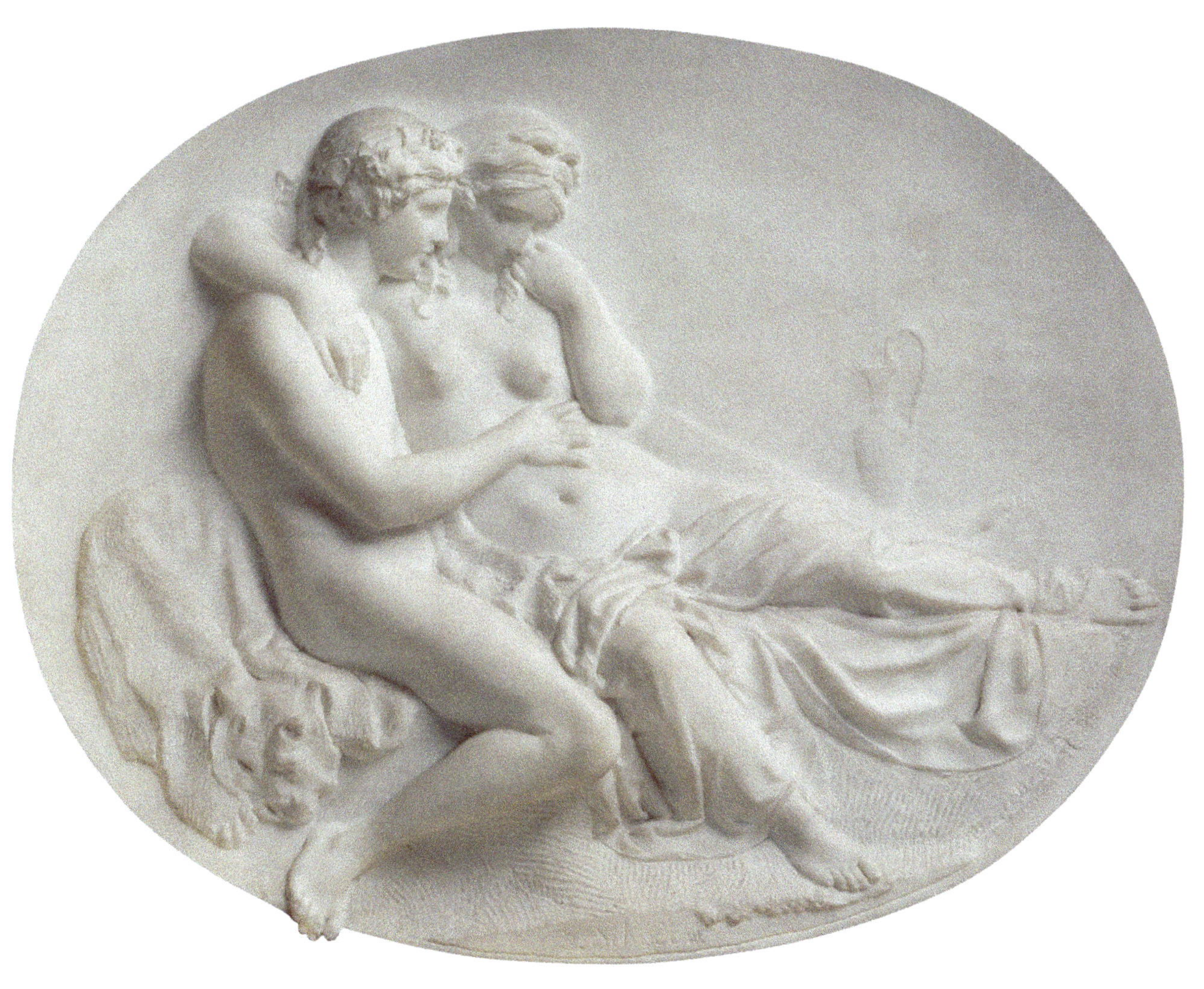

▲ **Johann Gottfried Schadow**,
Bacchus Comforting Ariadne, 1793.
Neoclassicism. Marble.
Hamburger Kunsthalle, Hamburg.

of the virtuous new French regime. Neoclassicism had other more specific causes, a renewed interest in antiquity, which was fueled by the discovery and excavation of Herculaneum (1738), as well as the growing trend of aristocrats and the educated classes of Europe to make a 'Grand Tour' of travel through Europe, but to Italy in particular. This travel and learning experience was particularly focused on the arts of Italy from antiquity and the Renaissance.

The shattering political events of the late eighteenth century and early nineteenth century occurred during the flowering of Neoclassicism, but the origins of that style preceded the American (1775 – 1783) and French (1789-1792) Revolutions and also helped to create an appeal for a new style: Neoclassicism. Flourishing, it is true, in America and in France, Neoclassicism was equally at home in England, Russia, and Sweden, and it had reverberations in such places as Italy, Austria, Mexico, and elsewhere throughout the western world. It was manifested in all of the arts, including sculpture and its siblings, architecture and the decorative arts.

The neoclassical style is characterized by moral content, strong, clear compositions, and often appeals to patriotic virtue. Napoleon Bonaparte (1769 – 1821) filled the power gap in the revolutionary chaos by ascending to power and crowning himself emperor of France in 1804. He too, embraced the neoclassical style as it created a symbolic system to bolster his authority, and he particularly favored connections to the Roman Empire in his expansionist phase of military conquest. The Neoclassicism produced a

fundamental change in the style and content of the visual arts throughout Europe and America.

Jacques Louis David (1748-1825) was the first man of genius to break with the traditions of the eighteenth century. A distant relative of Boucher, he was at first closely wrapped up in the teachings of this great man, although his own teacher, Joseph Marie Vien, had already begun to set out on a path of his own. David won the 'prix de Rome' when he was twenty-seven years old, and before setting out for Italy solemnly declared that the classic movement, which had begun with Winckelmann's publications in 1756, should not corrupt him. The antique, he said, « lacks action; it does not move». He had, however, hardly reached Rome when this maligned antique drew him into its nets and made him its most zealous proselyte. No other lover of the classic ideals has had such influence on art as David. He swept everything before him — France, Italy, Germany, and in part the Netherlands — and there is probably no country that has not felt the power of this painstaking and loving student of nature. « His one great fault,» says Professor Gensel, «was that he did not seek beauty in the individual, but in the average.» As a result, his art was not «natural and free, but cold and pedantic.» Cold it is, to be sure, but it is that coldness which suggests grandeur and nobility, and which compels the admiration of the spectator in spite of himself.

Nicolas de Courteille, ▶
Venus and Cupid, 1792. Neoclassicism.
Oil on canvas, 133 x 102 cm.
Sevastopol Art Museum, Sevastopol.

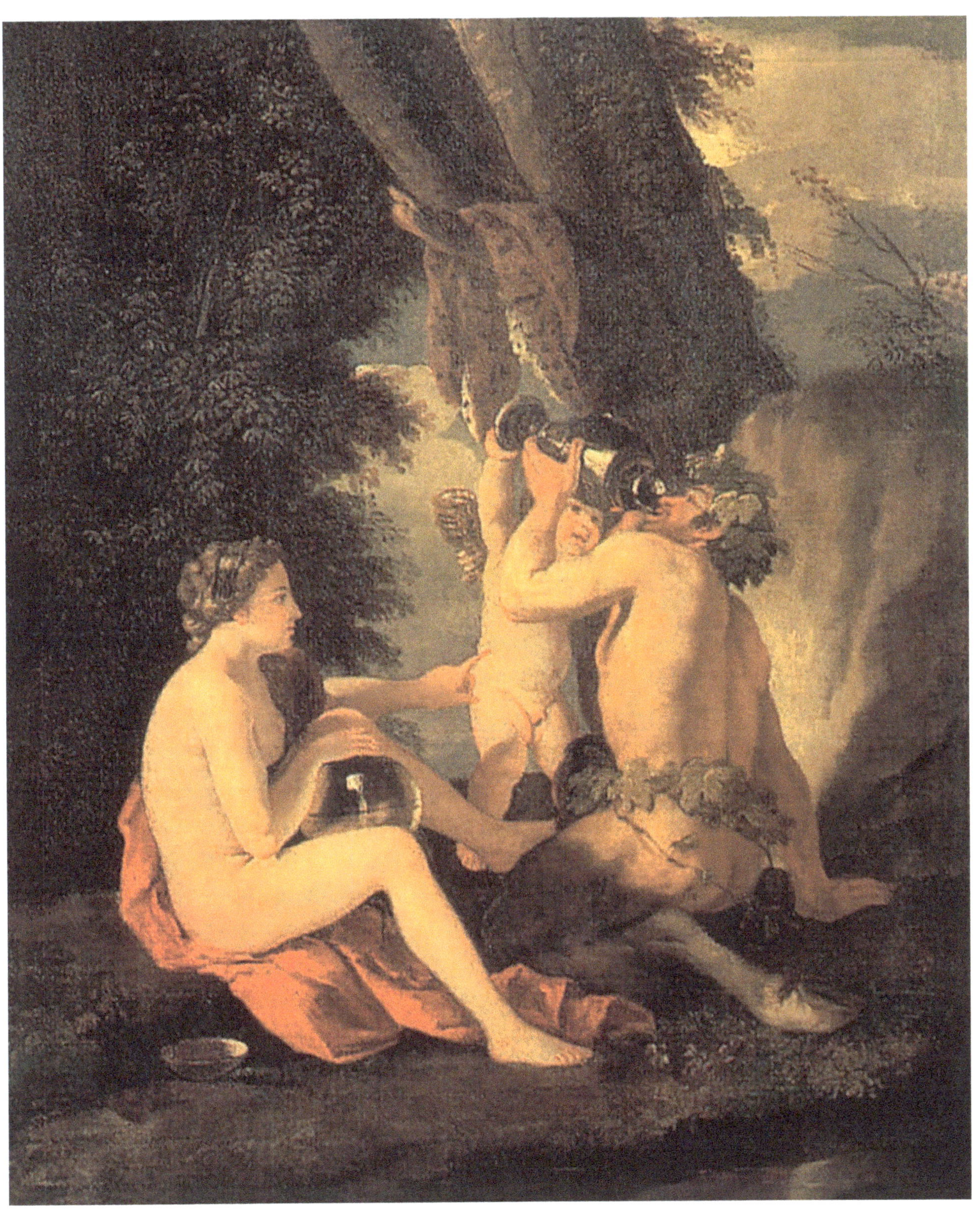

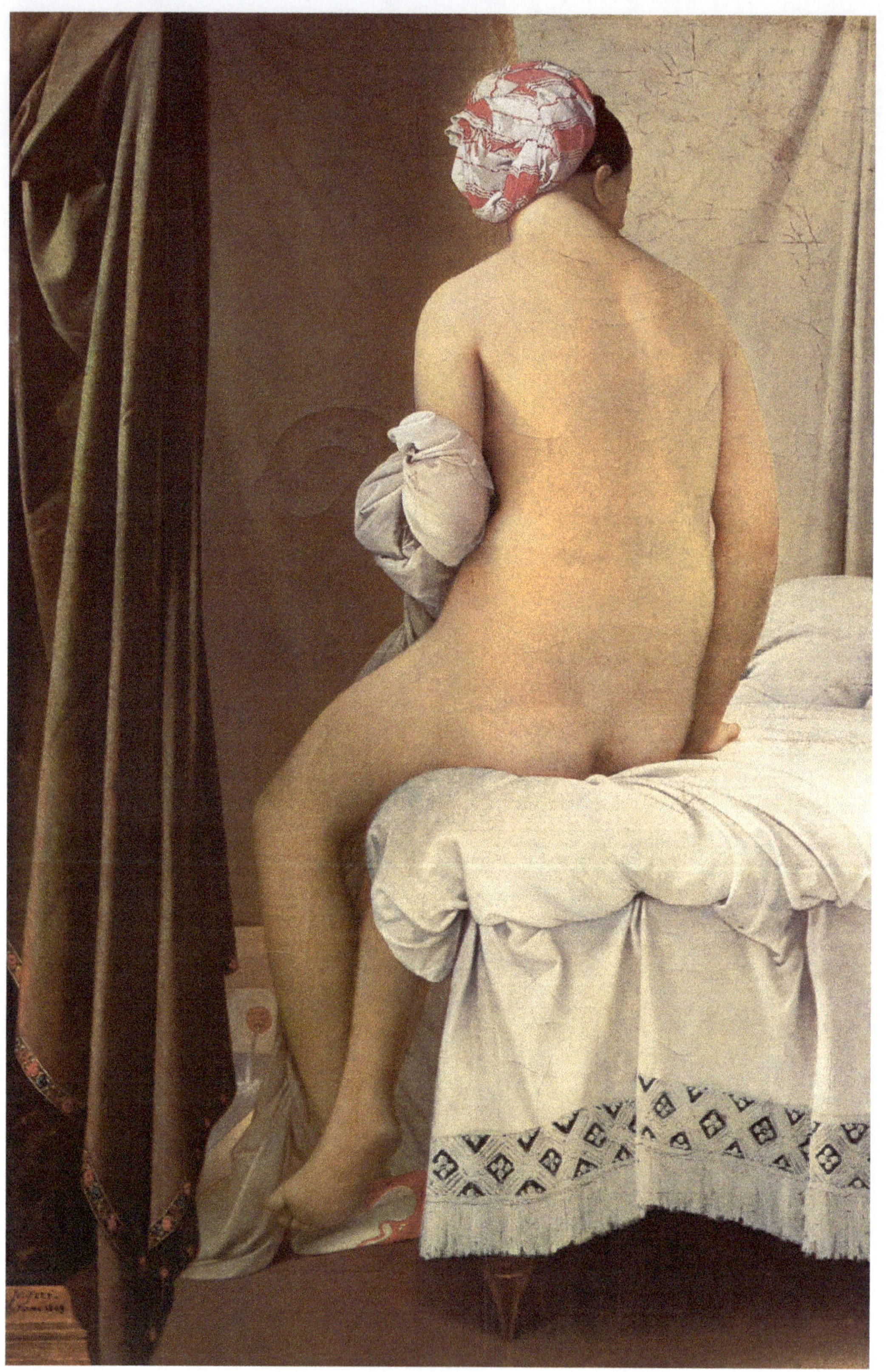

It is really with David that the century begins, for what preceded him was the art of the 'ancien regime' and of the Trianon. He had at the 'Century exhibition' a *Distribution of the Colors*, an *Ugolino*, some portraits; all of the most genuine David in choice of subject as well as treatment. Everywhere the capricious 'seeing yellow' which seems to have been a peculiarity of his eye; everywhere the grandly imposing, professorial infallibility of drawing which knows no first trying, no anxious searching, no hot struggle with the never quite attainable Nature. David compels with an imperious Medusa-glance the ever-stirring, the ever-flowing, so that it becomes fixed, and he can shackle the now immovable vision in brazen outlines. So, his human beings appear statues, or mimes, which maintain a pose, and his most blameless anatomies acquire a tendency towards the artificial. David's mood is always uniformly high-pitched. Good-humored people, who would like to see the majestic man in shirt sleeves for once, lurk in vain for him to unbutton himself. He never forsakes the decoration and costume of high tragedy.

At first, he sought the drama in ancient history or world-famed poetry. Afterwards, he found it in his immediate surroundings. Fate vouchsafed him the favor of living in a time, the pathos of which was mightier than that of Athens, Sparta, or Rome. He satisfied his deepest longings

 Jean-Auguste Dominique Ingres,
The Bather, known as *The Valpinçon Bather*, 1808.
Neoclassicism. Oil on canvas, 146 x 97.5 cm.
Musée du Louvre, Paris.

when, in the *Sabine Women*, he preached to the murderous factions among his people reconciliation and brotherly love, and, in *The Distribution of the Colors* and the *Coronation*, he made Napoleon the equal of the heroes of mythology. He is, therefore, always genuine, even when he may seem to the superficial gaze theatrical. It is the difference between a tone naturally sustained during moments of life at high pressure, and declamation learned from a teacher of rhetoric.

Although much had been discovered at that time, the works from which David and Canova studied represented the decadence of Greek art; and thus, we find in David's pictures a somewhat affected and effeminate type of figure. From these studies, he learned to draw accurately, but he never so thoroughly mastered the real spirit of his models as to be able to give life and action to his figures. He painted scenes like the *Sabine Women*, taken from classical antiquity, but they are wanting in life and reality. David's really great merit is not so much in what he achieved himself, as in having broken away from the affectations and the indecency of the preceding generation, and in having taught his successors to draw with severe accuracy — a lesson greatly needed — without imposing upon them his own faults and idiosyncrasies.

Of Neoclassical Inspiration

Of his pupils, Francois Gerard was the most famous, both for portraits and historical pictures. His best work, the *Entry of Henry IV into Paris*, is excellently grouped, accurately drawn, and shows great ability in the variety of expressions on the faces. Of the contemporaries of David, several followed the classical tendency, but without carrying it to the same excess; of these, J. B. Regnault, P. N. Guerin, and P. P. Prudhon, were the most celebrated. Prudhon studied the works of Raphael and Correggio, and painted some charming pictures in imitation of the latter.

The reaction against the classical school in favor of an art more directly inspired by life and nature, and more in harmony with the spirit of the age, began among David's own pupils. The romantic movement in literature began within a few years of the fall of the empire, and went on growing till the middle of the century under the leadership of Victor Hugo. The first impulse showed itself in Baron Gros, a pupil of David, who, beginning by clothing classical figures in modern dress, came to exhibit in his work a high degree of life and movement. This is to be seen at its best in the pictures of the Napoleonic wars — *Napoleon visiting the Plague-stricken Soldiers at Jaffa* and *Napoleon at Eylau*. In the former, the contrasts of color between the brilliant uniform and the pallid features of the sufferers is most striking, and the energy of expression remarkable.

Baron Gros, on the death of David, in 1825, accepted the headship of his school, and returned to his master's manner. Theodore Géricault, whose famous picture of the *Raft of the Medusa* strikes every visitor to the Louvre, returned to the study of nature without altogether breaking away from the tradition of David. In the figures of the dying and suffering men, we can see both the vivid study of nature and passion, and the influence of the Greek ideal.

His pupils, imitators, and rivals have, on the contrary, not succeeded in avoiding declamation. Gerard, Gros, Riesener, and Drolling were, consciously or unconsciously, the greatest flatterers that ever-painted portraits. Because David represented Napoleon in the character of an Alexander of Macedon, or an ancient god of war, the others, the smaller painters, in their portraits gave to even the ordinary men of the period the deportment of Olympian gods. Only Gerard's *Letitia* who, too, bore apotheosis most easily, is a good modest human being. All the other women are Juno or Pallas Athene; all the men Mars or Achilles. The contrast between the commonplace physiognomies and the magnificence of their appearance is now and then so violent that one is led to surmise that the painter wanted to make fun of his models. *Charles X. in his Coronation Robes*, by Ingres, seems, for example, virtually a parody of David's Coronation *of Napoleon*.

Gericault stands an examination of his title to fame badly. He has not so correct an eye for the figures of horses as was believed before instantaneous photographs. His portraits of soldiers are really more crude than powerful. Even the sketch for *the Raft of the Medusa*, reveals evidence of straining after effect which our pious admiration refused to notice in the colossal work in the Louvre. On the other hand, the figure of Louis Leopold Boilly gained strangely in the 'Century Exhibition'. Up till then, only his Arrival *of a Diligence at a Posting- house*, in the

Marie-Guillemine Benoist, ▶
Portrait of a Negress, 1800.
Neoclassicism. Oil on canvas, 81 x 65 cm.
Musée du Louvre, Paris.

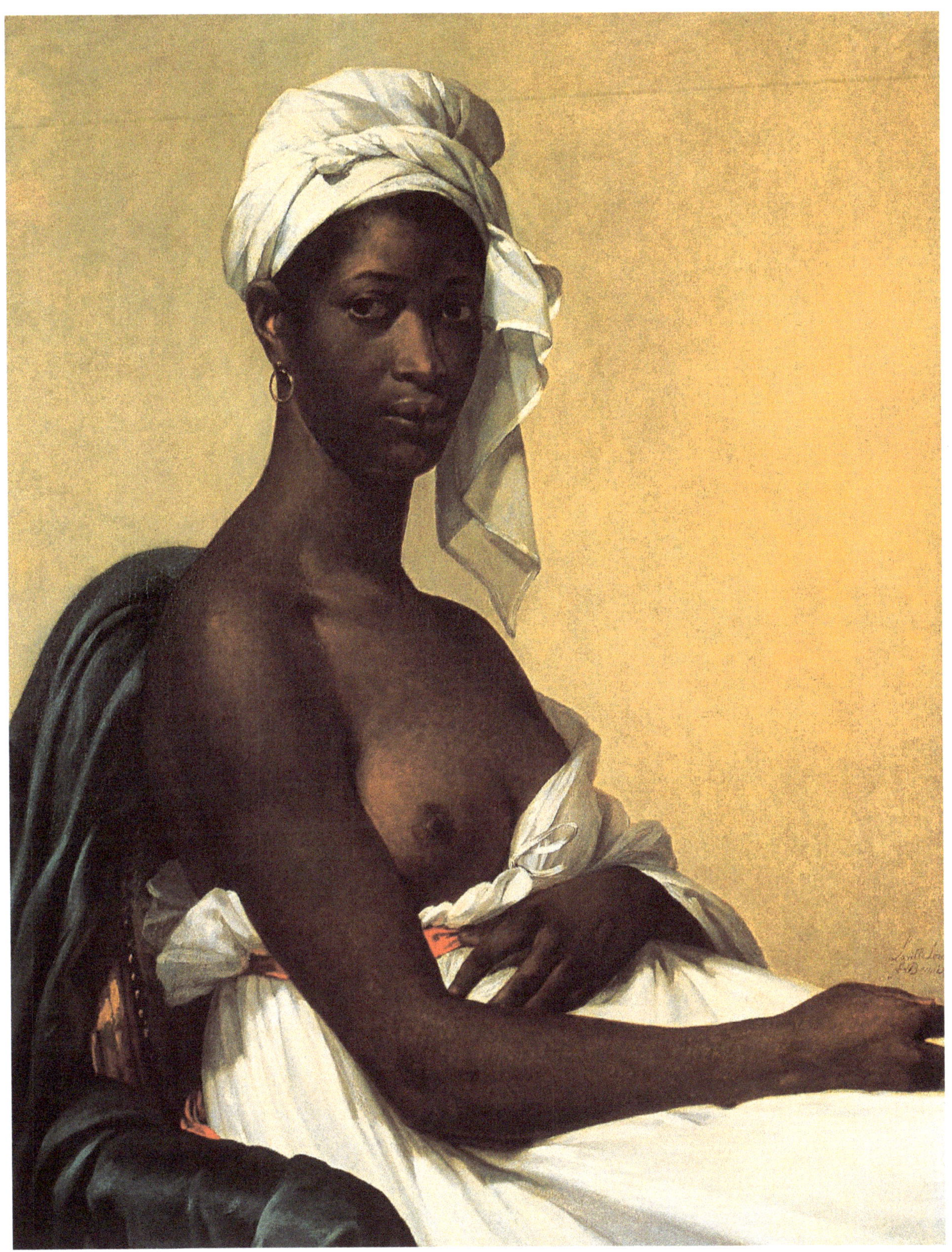

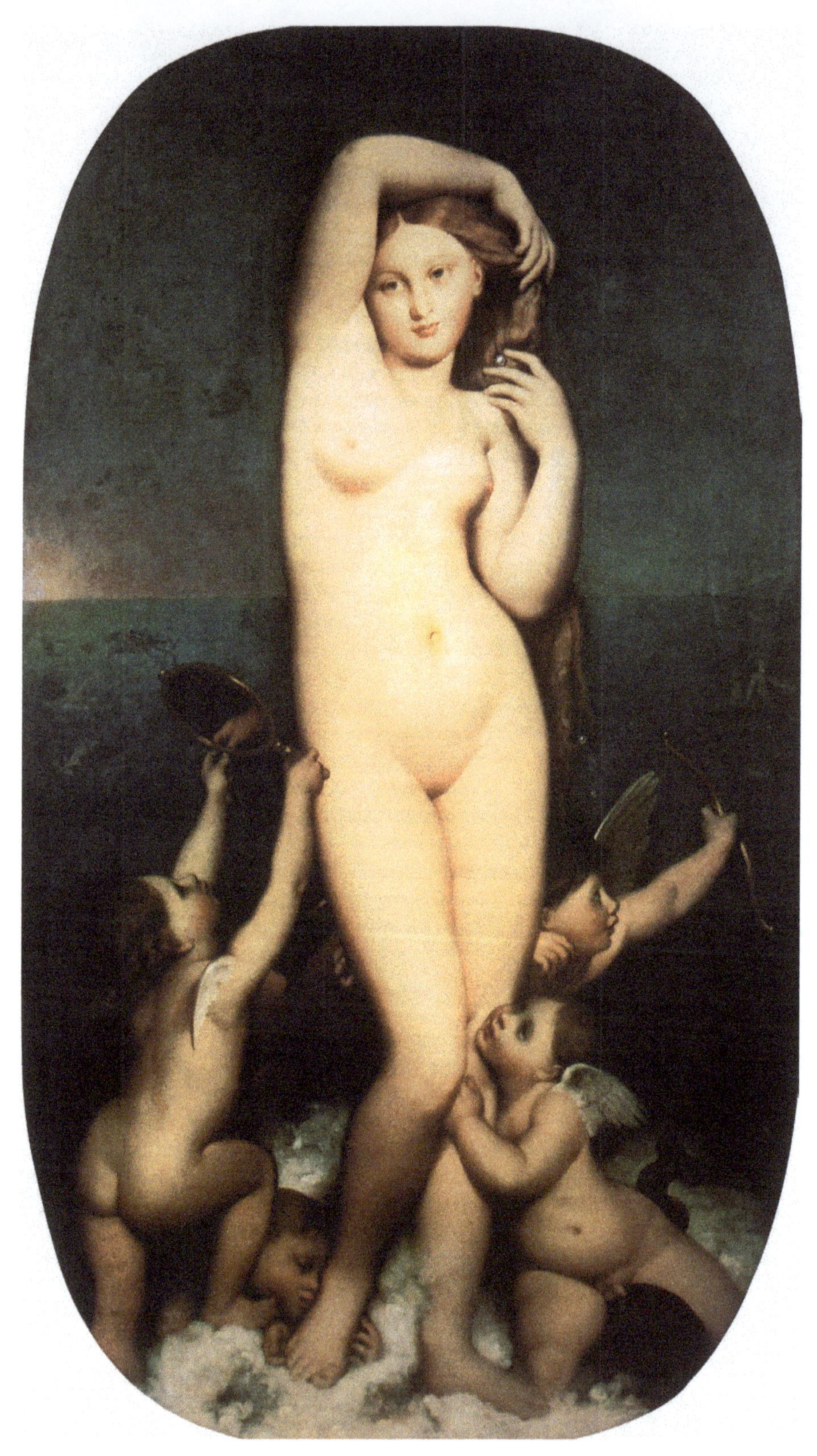

Louvre was known, and one did not rate him very highly on account of the affected atelier light of this otherwise prettily studied little picture. Here he disclosed himself as a great philosopher and satirist. One picture represents a popular merry-making with wine gratis another a free performance at the 'Ambigu – Comique Theater'. There the crowd is fighting murderously over a drink that can be had for nothing; half-grown hobbledehoys throttle bestial graybeards; bullies claw hold of furies; dreadful feet trample on faces and necks in the mad storming of the wine supplies, and the victors in this struggle have their reward: they lie on the ground bestially drunk. The scenes at the entrance of the theater are not quite so vulgar. There is a less dogged scramble for intellectual enjoyment than for that of the palate. Yet here, too, the most brutal lack of consideration and greedy selfishness triumph; here, too, the strong man overmasters the weak; here, too, among beings who seem to belie their human form, the law of the jungle holds good; and here, too, poor people pay for a little doubtful pleasure with the sufferings, dangers, and exertions of a storming of the Malakoff.

Neoclassicism elsewhere the world

There are few illustrations of a neoclassical tidal wave which swept over all parts of the world that came under the influence of Europe. Thus, in the midst of a century of revolutions we see the curiously paradoxical situation of artists looking to the past while being carried along the current toward a new age. This was due partly to the romantic movement, which whetted the appetite for a deeper understanding of the past and set it up as a summum bonum. In addition, as there had not yet emerged a new age coherent enough to manifest itself, the disintegrating Renaissance revealed its decadence, as is normal, in an archaistic expression.

That classicism took so strong a hold on the youthful United States is due partly to the wave of nationalism which permeated the country and demanded a break artistically as well as politically with England; and partly to the influence of Thomas Jefferson, who saw in pure classicism a style which seemed to answer that demand.

Four hundred and twenty artists of all nationalities are mentioned as pupils of David; few, however, have made names for themselves. The personality of the master was too powerful. As a result, his school soon declined, and would have done so even sooner if Jean Dominique Ingres (1780-1867) had not infused new life into it. Ingres was attracted not only by the antique but also by the later paintings of Raphael, which taught him grace. His color was always subservient to his drawing. The fact that Ingres sought inspiration in part from Raphael makes a bond between the classic movement under his leadership and the so-called Romanticists, for these men also turned to the masters of a more immediate past.

The classic enthusiasm kindled among German artists in the eighteenth century by Carstens

◀ **Jean-Auguste Dominique Ingres**,
Venus Anadyomene, 1808 and 1848. Neoclassicism.
Oil on canvas.
Musée Condé, Chantilly.

and Mengs continued in the early nineteenth century with Genelli, Preller, and Rottmann, all of whom sought inspiration in the study of the antique. Genelli (1798 -1868) was the only one of this trio who was not interested in landscapes. His forte was the human figure, especially in motion. In the best works by Preller (1804-1878) the figures are only insignificant parts of the picture. Often, they are disturbing, for Preller did not know how to make them necessary to his compositions. He was a man of vivid imagination, who in his mind peopled the rocks and coasts which he studied on a journey to Naples, and drew from them his famous illustrations to the Odyssey, Rottmann (1797-1850) was the greatest of the heroic landscapists, but he also suffered at times from the erroneous notion that a landscape without figures cannot arouse in the spectator proper emotions. Without being familiar with the much later school of open-air artists, he delighted in phases of nature which are characteristic of them — sunsets, storms, and moonlight. With him they were means of appealing to the emotions, owing to the things which they suggested — the grandeur of nature and the mystery of life. The open-air painters resort to them because of the studies in light and shade which they enable them to make, and the resulting color schemes.

In all their works, the German Classicists are clearly distinguished from their contemporary Frenchmen known by the same name. Both received their inspiration from the antique, but while the Germans endeavored to sink themselves into the spirit of antiquity, the Frenchmen learned from ancient art their fine technique. With them it was the how, with the Germans the what, that mattered most.

It was largely the classic school of David, which had begun to find ardent admirers also in Italy. Appiani (1754-1817) of Milan espoused its cause, and, being a man of considerable worth, succeeded in painting pictures, which even today deserve praise. Other artists, such as Coghetti (1804-1 875) of Rome, sought inspiration in contact with the German Romanticists, the best of whom then lived in Rome. The Classicists and the Romanticists alike were attracted by historical subjects, so that historic and historical-religious pictures were the best to be found in Italy in the first half of the nineteenth century.

With the dawn of the nineteenth century the long Flemish sleep of artistic inactivity which had followed upon the death of Rubens ended. David, woke the people from their lethargy. He was a born leader, so that the Belgian artists, naturally flocked about him when after the fall of Napoleon, he settled among them an exile. The Belgian national sympathies, however, were not with the classic tendencies which David represented. When once the Belgians had received from him their incentive to art, they soon turned to their own master, Rubens, for inspiration. They did this the more eagerly

Pierre Narcisse Guérin, ▶
Aurora and Cephalus, 1811-1814. Neoclassicism.
Oil on canvas, 257 x 178 cm.
The Pushkin State Museum of Fine Arts, Moscow.

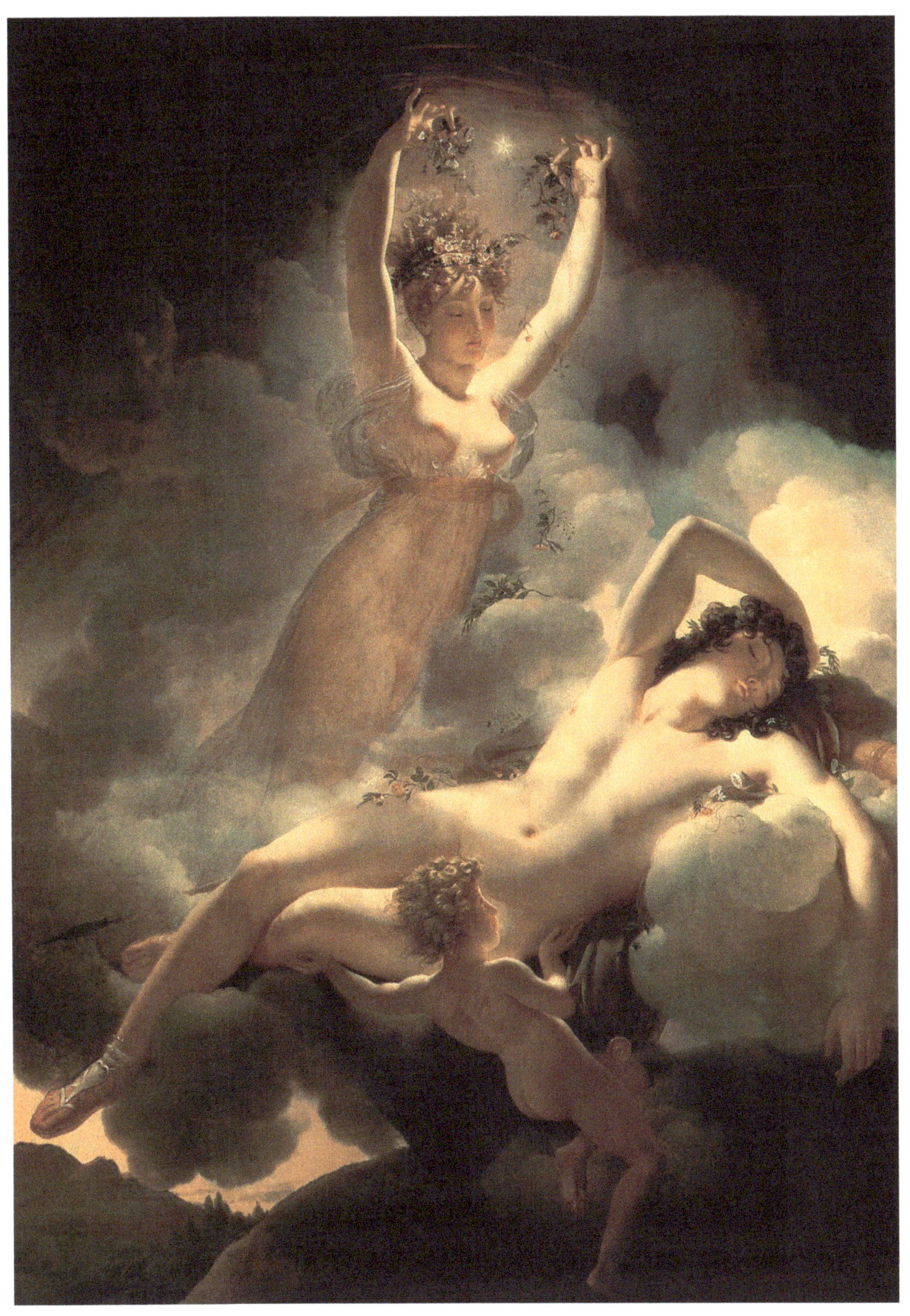

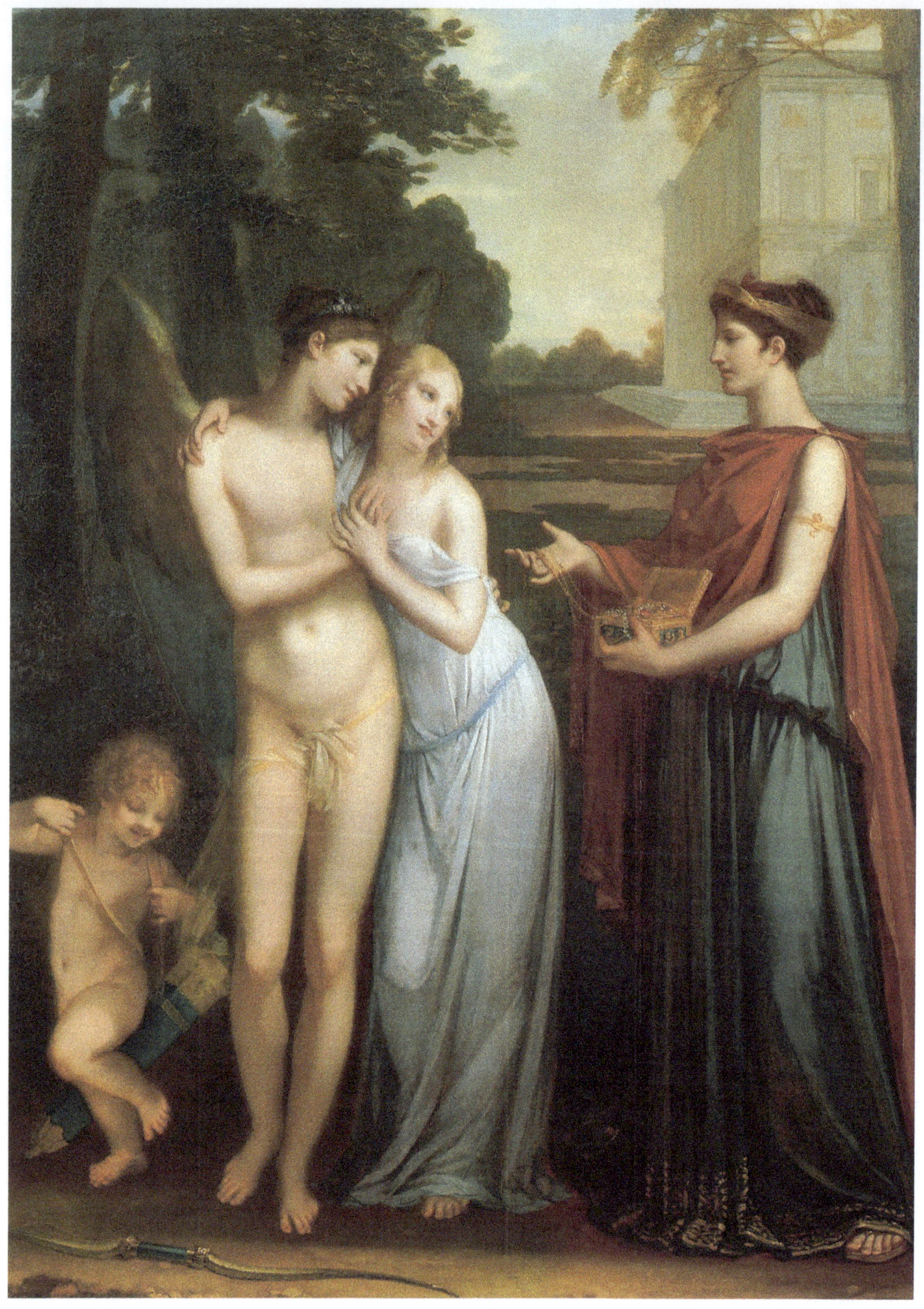

because their country in 1830 had declared its political independence, and a newly born patriotism had taken hold of the people. Soon an era of historical painting began. Huge canvases were filled with scenes taken from the history of the nation. Hugeness and accuracy of drawing do not go hand in hand. Color, however, lends itself well to the decoration of large-sized canvases. Color, moreover, had been the distinctive mark of Rubens, and as such made a sentimental appeal to the people, not to mention the fact that their national character is probably such that it is better able to appreciate the beauty of color than that of line.

The nineteenth century did not open auspiciously for Dutch art. The level was low, yet not so low that a reversion to better things followed as a necessary conclusion. The powerful personality of David of France made itself felt also in Holland; but neither the artists nor the public took kindly to the principles and ideas of his classic school. Classicism, therefore, has hardly a place in the history of Dutch art.

◀ **Pierre Paul Prud'Hon** and
Constance Mayer-Lamartinière,
Innocence Preferring Love over Wealth, 1804. Neoclassicism.
Oil on canvas, 243 x 194 cm.
The State Hermitage Museum, St Petersburg.

▼ **Augustin Pajou,**
Psyche Abandoned, 1785-1790. Neoclassicism.
Marble, height: 177 cm.
Musée du Louvre, Paris.

Sculpture

The Italian Antonio Canova, working for an international clientele, flattered Napoleon with grand, ideal nude (now in the courtyard of the Brera Museum), and in a memorable image of Napoleon's sister, Pauline Borghese.

The seminude Pauline with Grecian profile reminiscent of a Venus, is recumbent on classical-revival furniture copied from ancient Roman design.

The Englishman Joseph Wilton and the American Horatio Greenough contributed in their own ways to the same rediscovery of the ideals of classical sculpture, a movement that started as a slight on the frivolities of the Rococo and ended as one of the continuing revival movements of the nineteenth century.

The international quality of the style is shown in the works of Bertel Thorvaldsen, who, like most fellow neoclassical painters and sculptors of the time, rendered his subjects with gentle emotional sentiment and soft surface texture.

Whether fairly or unfairly, the nineteenth century is not usually seen as a great century of sculpture. The same cannot be said for the 20th century, when the art form was often practiced went hand in hand with painting in finding expression in innovative styles.

▼ **Johann Gottfried Schadow,**
The Crown Princesses Louise and Friedrike of Prussia, 1796-1797. Neoclassicism.
Marble, height: 172 cm. Alte Nationalgalerie, Berlin.

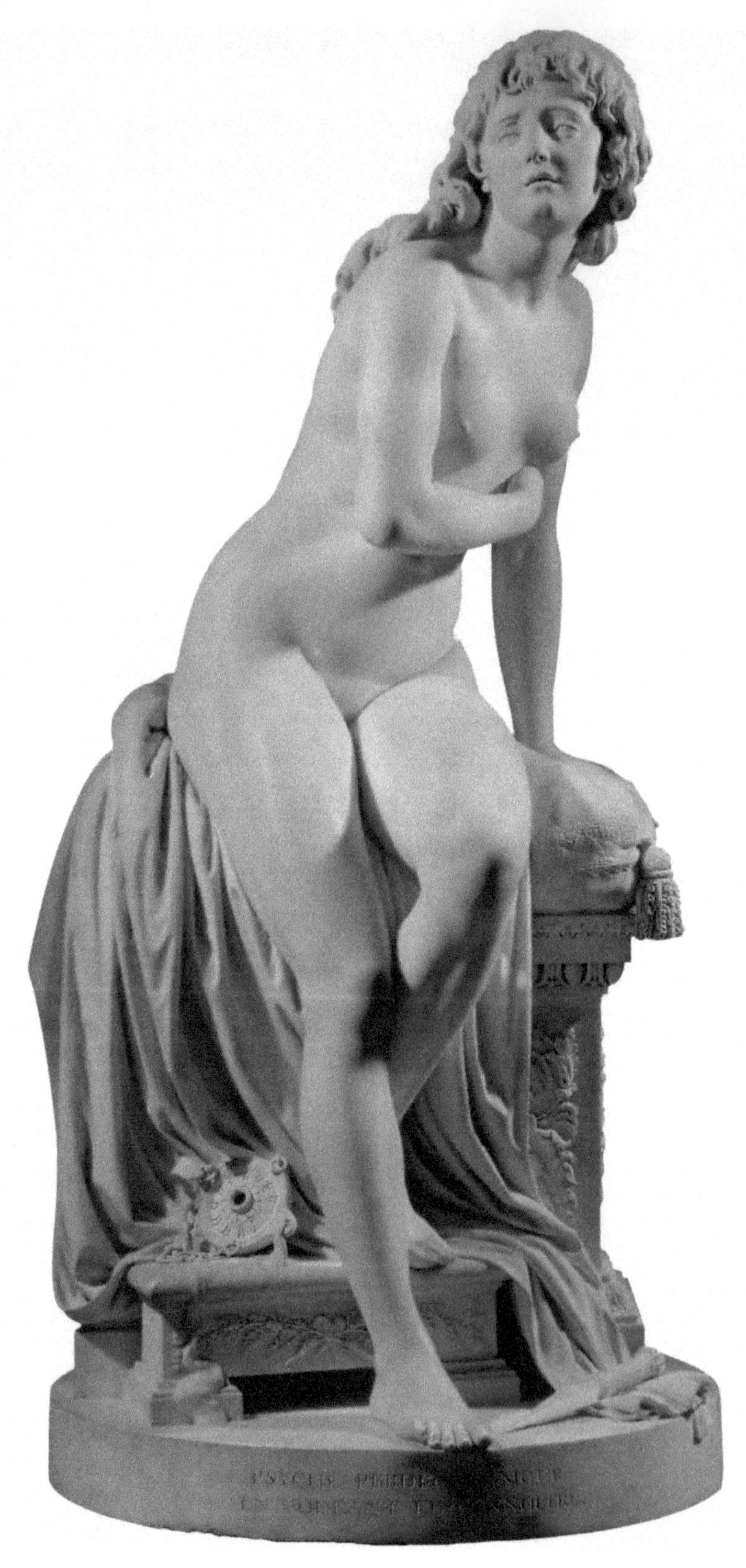

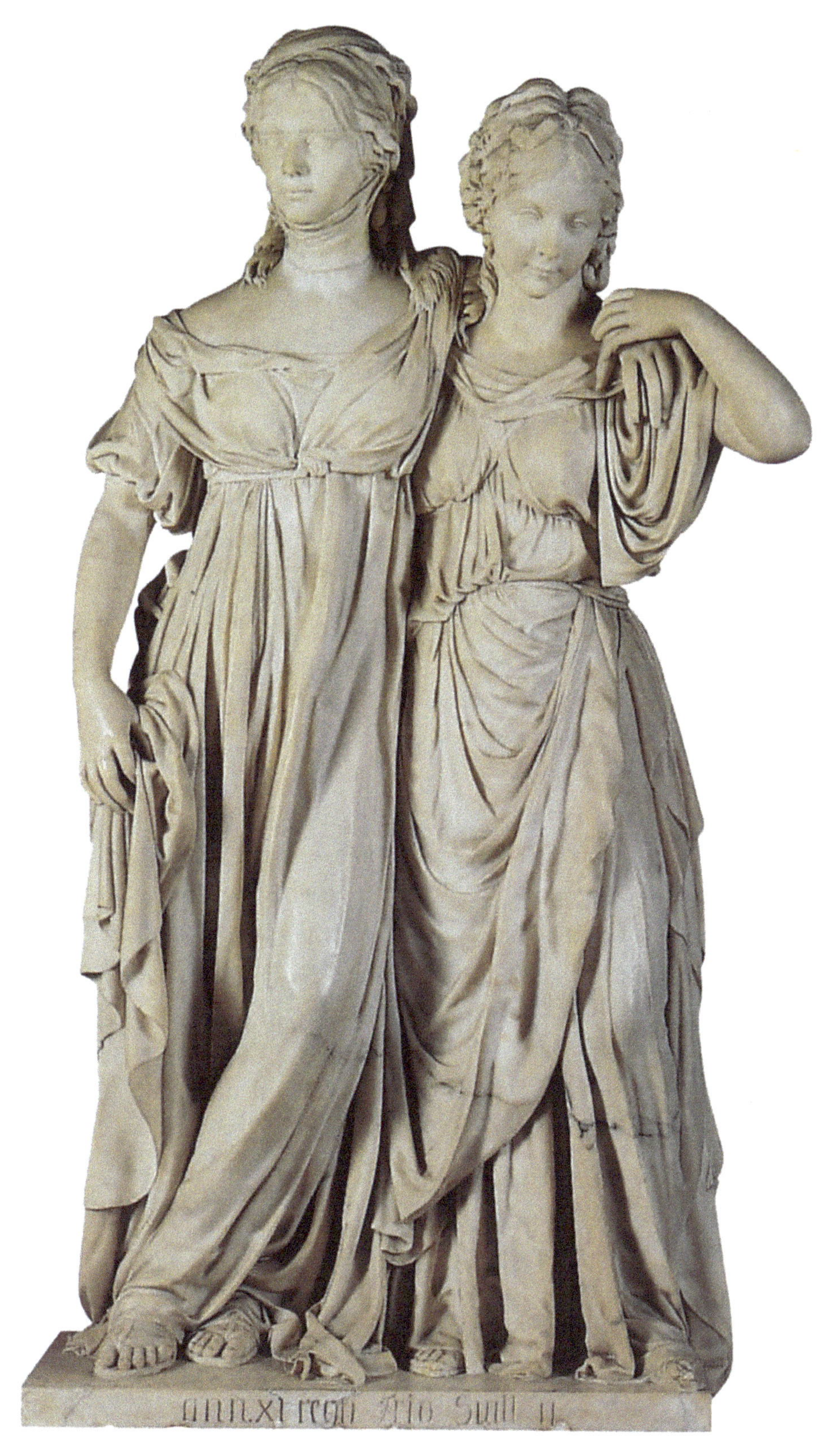

Architecture

The Enlightenment saw the emergence of a new kind of architectural treatise in Europe, one that was less technical and more theoretical or speculative in nature, and which attempted to reconcile the new faith in reason with the traditional reliance on Classical precedent. Most notable here is the *Essay on Architecture* (1753) of Abbot Laugier, who put forward the idea that the Classical system derived from the most ancient building type, a hypothetical construction of tree trunks which has often been termed the 'primitive hut'. This entirely conjectural proposal served to anchor Classicism in both reason and nature, thus ensuring its continuing intellectual attractiveness. Other writers of a Neoclassical persuasion continued to subject Classicism to the new forces of reason, a process which nevertheless acted only to reinforce its supremacy. This was further confirmed by the many folio volumes of etchings put out by the Venetian architect Giovanni Battista Piranesi, who aimed to demonstrate the superiority of Roman architecture solely on the basis of its great size, complexity and engineering prowess. Almost unwittingly, however, Piranesi's unforgettably dense and moody depictions of the monumental ruins of Rome also served to affirm that Classical architecture could be turned to ends of pure emotion rather than strict rationalism, thus laying the ground for the Romanticism of Soane, Ledoux, Boullée, Schinkel and others.

The 19th century nevertheless witnessed new challenges to the classical monopoly from architects who espoused a return to medieval building practices. This initiative was taken, as often as not, on the basis of moral or religious principles rather than on technical grounds. John Ruskin, who had no professional or technical training in building whatsoever, proposed that the most important aspect of architecture was its ornamentation, which could engage the uncoerced and creative talents of a variety of people in society. His model was the Gothic churches and cathedrals of Europe, and most particularly the highly ornate and colorful version of Gothic to be found in Venice. As laid out in his *Seven Lamps of Architecture* (1849) and *The Stones of Venice* (1851-1853), Ruskin's emphasis on the dignity of the craft traditions was soon to inspire many writers and practitioners of the Arts and Crafts school, led by the socialist philosopher William Morris.

The Expressive Moods of Neoclassicism

The new order is offered the tool which it demands. For a quarter of a century, Antiquity has been before the minds of men. That way lies Virtue, and there also is Beauty. André Chenier dedicates hymns to David, in whose works Robespierre recognizes the physical expression of that which he himself represents in the moral world; and it is to David that the Convention entrusts the work of organizing Republican aesthetics on the model of the austerity, the pomp and the stoicism of

Antonio Canova, ▶
Tomb of Archduchess Marie-Christine of Austria, 1798-1805.
Neoclassicism. Marble, height: 574 cm.
Augustinerkirche, Vienna. In situ.

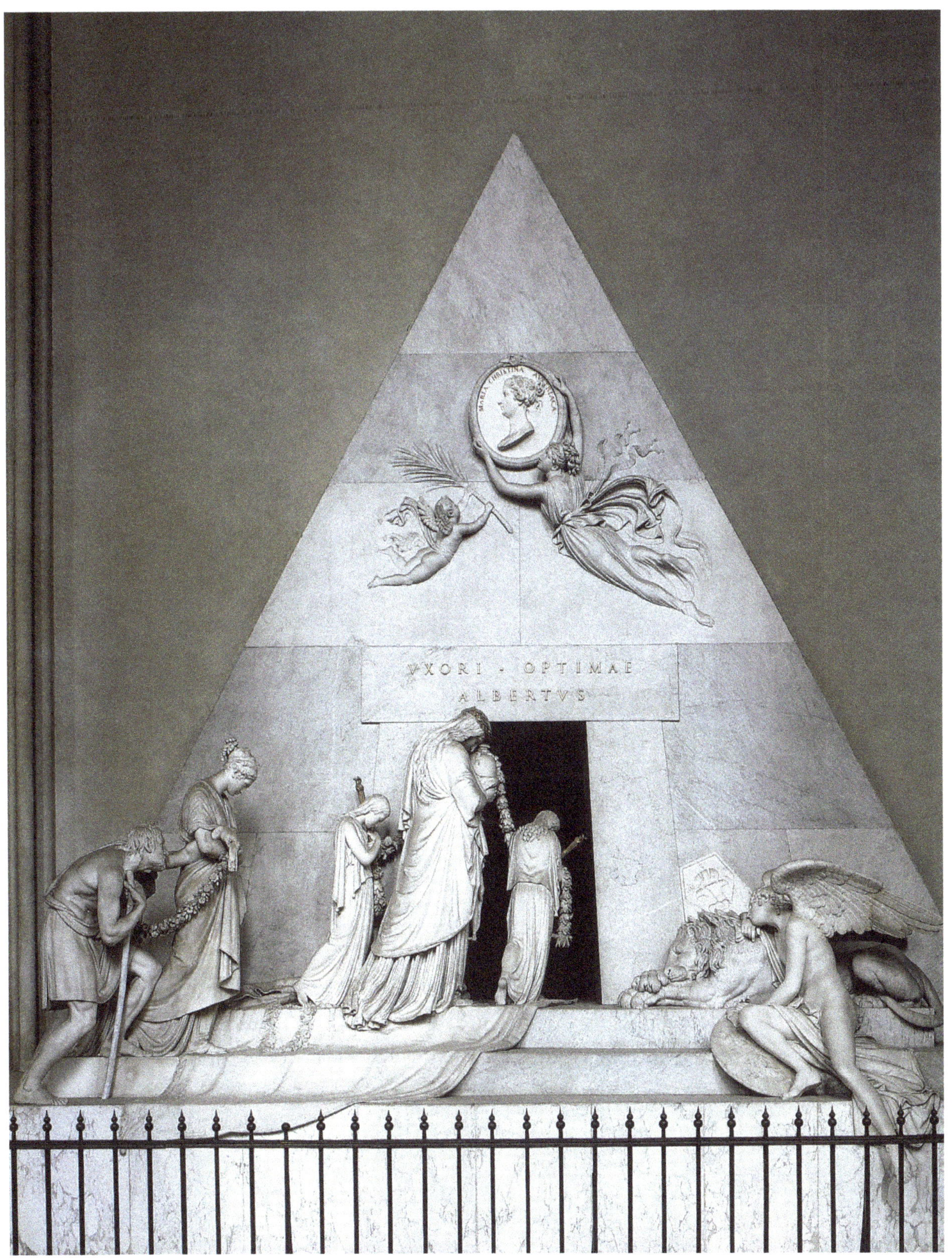
MARIA CHRISTINA AVGVSTA
VXORI · OPTIMAE
ALBERTVS

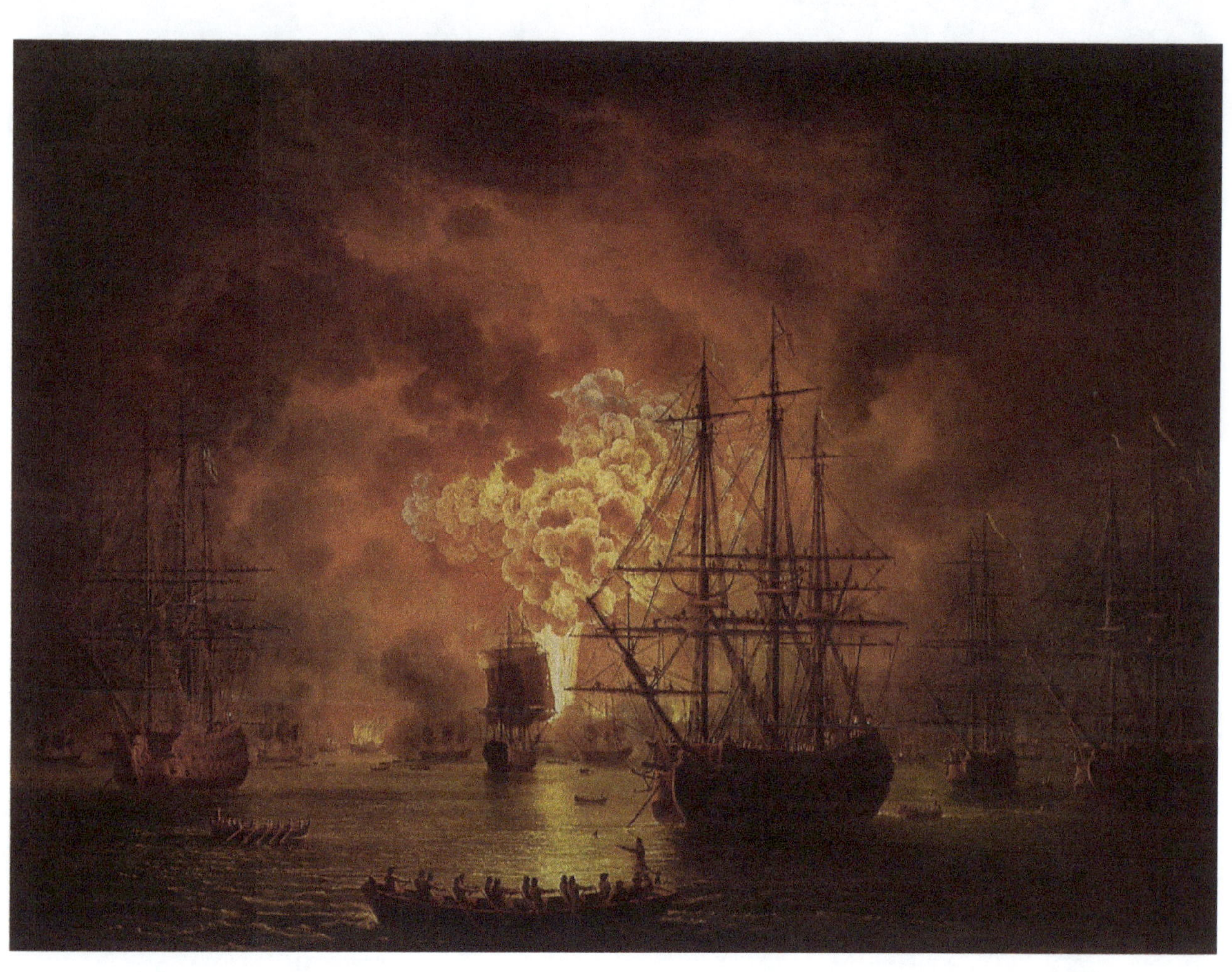

Rome. David's education as a painter and as a man has prepared him to become the Le Brun of the Revolution.

As a winner of "The Prix de Rome" David finds Rome filled with the fever or archaeology. Less than twenty years before, there had occurred the discovery of the mummified cities, Herculaneum and Pompeii. Piranesi's engravings circulate everywhere arid animate the ruins of Rome with a somber and living spirit, Hubert Robert haunts the crumbling walls there, the unequal colonnades the broken vaults covered by ivy and grass, and all the fields of dead stones where the ground, as its level rises, still gives a glimpse, here and there, of half-buried gods. Joseph Vernet descends from the two emigrants of the great century, Le Lorrain and Poussin. Since the time when Giambattista Vico created the philosophy of History, the very soil of Italy seems to awaken adjusted to the understanding of the ladies of easy virtue, of the diplomats, and the litterateurs. The Germans seek to found a science of aesthetics on the basis of a Greco-Latin archeology that is insufficiently understood. Winkelmann has just written his *History,* Lessing, publishes a whole volume of the tiresome *Laocoön.* In France, besides, where Montesquieu by his *Grandeur et Decadence des Romains* pointed the road long ago, where Soufflot is building the Pantheon, where the 'Encyclopédie'

◄ **Jacob Philipp Hackert,**
1737-1807, Neoclassicism, German,
The Destruction of the Turkish Fleet in Chesme Harbour, 1771.
Oil on panel, 162 x 220 cm.
The State Hermitage Museum, St Petersburg.

has had to search the ancient world through and through, and where Caylus, a man of taste, to whom the artists lent a willing ear, is writing innumerous memoirs on the sculptured stones and the medals.

A nephew of Boucher, and loving Fragonard, issuing from them and retaining their imprint, David sees clearly that if their century still kept some reflection of living life, it is to them that it owes it, to them who, after all, represent the direct descent from Watteau and from Rubens. It is in their name that he so harshly combats the Academy, which the Convention suppresses as soon as he demands it. But between them and him there is the distance between the conversationalists and the journalists who prepare the revolution and those who made it. They destroyed; he constructs. As he thinks to rediscover in the Roman marbles the discipline he needs in order to look truth in the face, he goes straight ahead to it, his head down, and his back turned on the men and the things of his time. He does not see that he is falling into the same error as the School which he execrates.

His whole life, thenceforward, will be a stubborn and laborious collaboration between his nature as an artist and his will as an aesthetician, between the needs of his being and the beliefs of his time. He is a painter, as much as anyone can be. In those of his scenes from history in which the external movement is most closely copied from the ancient statues, in those of his pictures of the ceremonies of his time which are most directly brought back, by their cold, stiff arrangement, to the bas-reliefs of Roman arches, a purple robe, a cushion of blue velvet a golden embroidery, a plume, or a silk flag, everything connected with his immediate time, such as an accessory impossible to modify as to its material, is painted with the richest, densest, and most opaque splendor. Whenever he is not treating the nude body, the rigidity of the ensembles — always built up from without and by the processes of a technique interpreted according to its appearances and never according to its spirit — is sometimes forgotten before the intensity of the harmonies and the splendor of matter, which by an act of his will he deprives of its fire. One thinks of some Spanish painter of the seventeenth century, Zurbaran, for example, whose monk-like severity was no obstacle to his perceiving the thickness of fustian robes, the dense pallor of bread, the sonorous and hard grain of earthen pots, and even a certain silvery palpitation of the sky as it receded to the far horizon. And often he makes us think of some storyteller, robust and truculent, by the way he paints a rosy-faced church singer, or a fat-bellied canon, whom one must search out patiently in the least visible corner of some solemn canvas, but whom La Fontaine would find, and whom Courbet did not fail to see.

Almost always his will outstrips his sensibility, but sometimes it is the latter which forces the former to retreat. How many portraits he has left unfinished, intentionally perhaps, the painter in him having been warned by his emotion at the instant when they were attaining their highest degree of power. Doubtless, he had, at such moments, the courage, so rare, of being stronger than one's principles and of halting in time. With their gray and troubled backgrounds and their hesitating pigment, with their expressive vigor and their fidelity, they seem as if suspended between the diffused life in which man's emotional existence begins, and consciousness in which his intellectual empire begins. They live, and yet their life remains between precise limits. They are built like monuments, and yet their surface moves. They breathe force and liberty at one and the same time. It is before them that one understands fully David's chagrin when, in 1816, he saw the marbles of the Parthenon. He felt that his career was a long misunderstanding, a permanent confusion between the truth which he encountered and the life which he had believed himself to be seizing.

He is deserving of respect. To be sure, he did not observe the terrible accent of the scenes in which he was often one of the actors. He did not hear the rolling sound of the wooden shoes as the women of the people marched along the pavement, nor the cannon that were defending the different sections of the city. He did not look at the livid heads on the points of the pikes, nor the red streams of blood. He did not listen to the storm rumbling in the breast of Danton. A member of the Convention, one would say that he did not live the tragedy of the Assembly. He did not feel the grand horror of war, nor shudder to have the archangel before his eyes. No matter. He is deserving of respect.

John Singleton Copley, ▶
1738-1815, Realism, American, *Watson and the Shark,* 1778.
Oil on canvas, 182.1 x 229.7 cm.
The National Gallery of Art, Washington D.C.

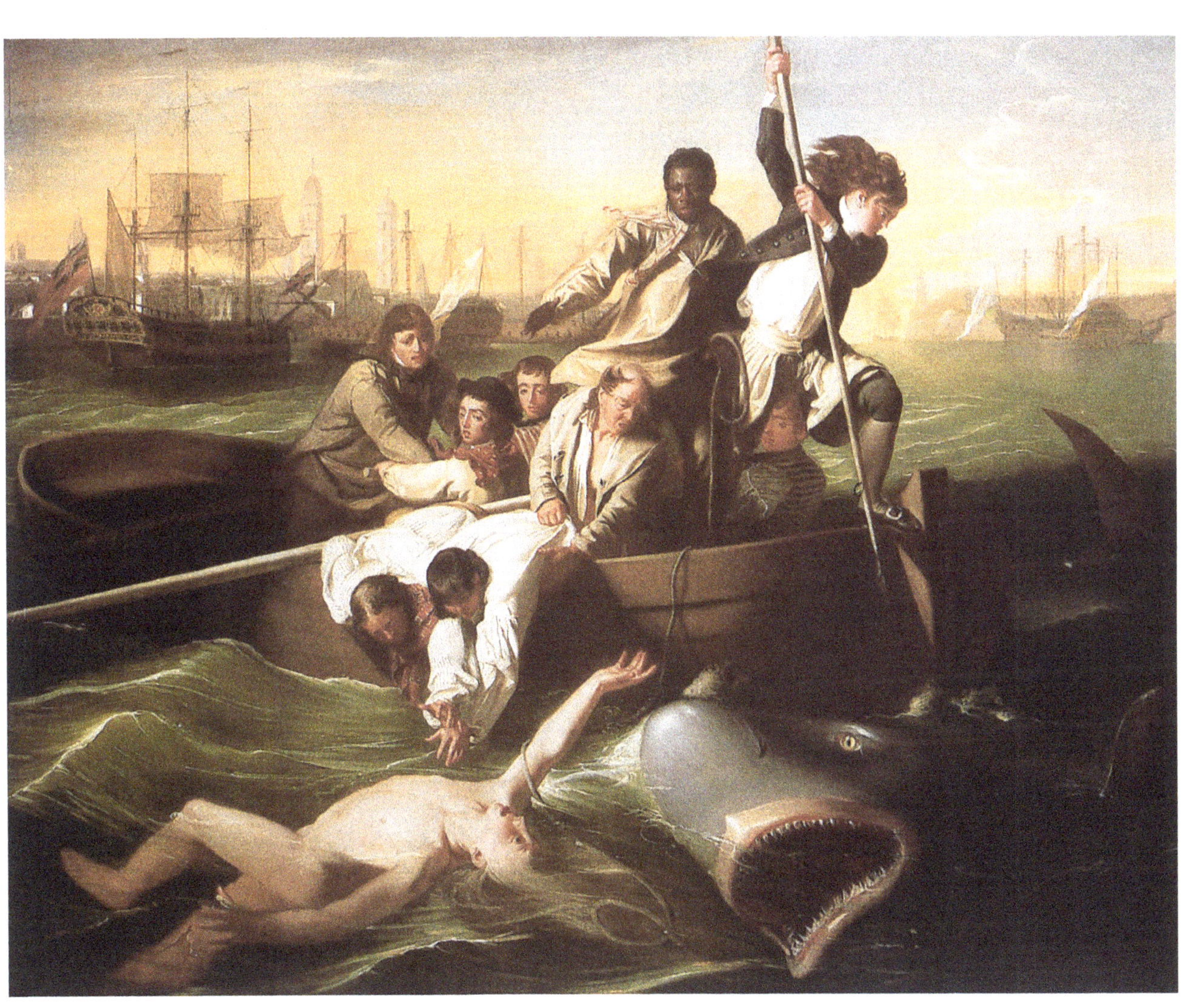

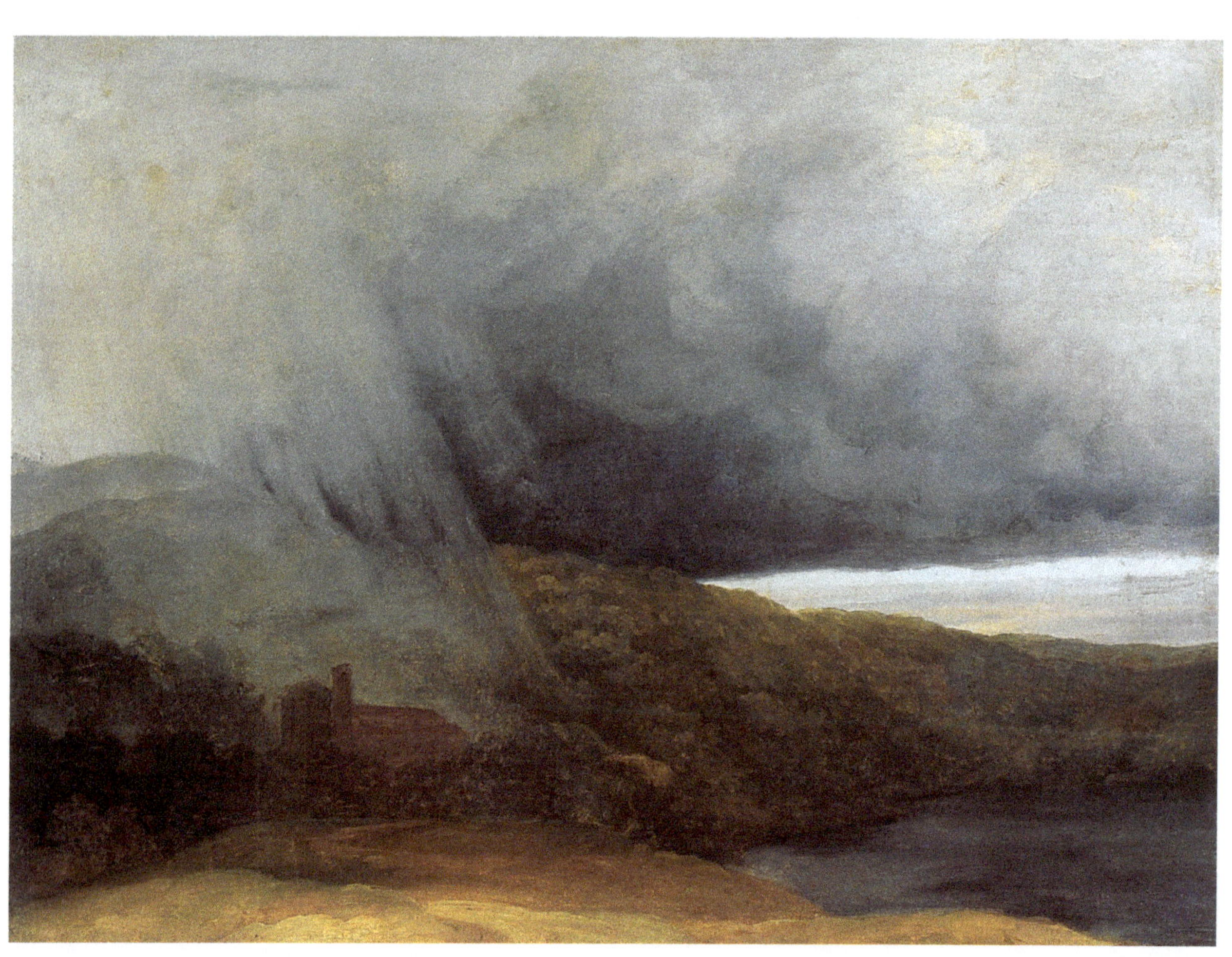

He restored to painted matter the substantiality which it had practically lost, and rehabilitated the religious and passionate spirit with which an artist should approach form and consider structure. He is, like the Revolution itself, practically intolerable in the letter, admirable in its intentions and its spontaneous movement. In his presence, one has the sensation of a people regaining control of itself. Everything before him is talk, frivolity, and gossip. Introduced by Rousseau into artistic activity' as the Jacobin was introduced into political activity, he comes, stirs minds, and tries to remake a world on the plane of the will. Grace flees, alas, and the remainder of life which it was dragging with it; but here is strength appearing, and here we catch a glimpse of truth. An abstract truth, outside of space, outside of the movement and the exchanges of life, to be sure, and corresponding to the abstract man. His aesthetics, it is true, resemble those constitutions drawn from Montesquieu and from Rousseau, borrowed from Geneva, London, or Rome, which jostled one another and tumbled over upon one another for ten years, giving France a political support which neither her aptitudes nor her temperament had prepared her to receive. No matter. During those essays at theory, the spirit of the Revolution, the spirit of life, was spreading over Europe with its armies, and mounting in the sentiment of everyone who was noble and strong.

◀ **Pierre Henri Valenciennes**,
1750-1819, Neoclassicism, French, *Storm by the Banks of a Lake*, Late 18th century.
Oil on canvas, 39.8 x 52 cm. Musée du Louvre, Paris.

The Decline

The Classical discipline, having been vigorously resisted by Romanticism, was no longer able to maintain its authority; and various other forms of art arose independently of it. Of these the most militant and aggressive has been Realism; and the most popular has been that kind of art to which contemporary French criticism has assigned the barbarous neologism, 'Modernity'.

In very many respects the history of art resembles the history of religion. When a discipline is universally accepted, or has a sufficient number of adherents to prevent the expression of other opinions, it acquires in the course of time such an appearance of permanence as to seem fixed and rooted in the very nature of things. But a time always arrives when the discipline is weakened from within; and not long afterwards some new idea, the germ of a new discipline, breaks forth into visible existence, even though merely to exist is in its case to be guilty of open rebellion. There is a close parallel between the history of Classicism and that of the Catholic Church. Romanticism, Realism, and Modernism are all Protestant; or, perhaps, a more accurate statement of the case would be this — Romanticism and Realism were Protestant, but Modernism is so entirely independent of Classicism as to have not even the idea of, protesting against it.

Meanwhile Classicism is forced to accept — which it does with loud complaints and many an anathema — the position of one of the art religions instead of the art religion; and it may maintain this kind of existence for a long time to come, shorn of all authority to punish heterodoxy, and compelled to see heterodoxy lifting its many heads in bold independence, yet still supported by venerable usage, and by the devotion of faithful adherents.

A discipline which has long exercised supreme power is seldom very justly estimated immediately after the overthrow of its supremacy. One thing in favor of it is, however, perfectly clear; we can all see that it was a true discipline, that it had definite purposes in culture, and trained men to these ends with elaborate care, and made them study patiently and long, comprehending perfectly the uses of culture, and willingly giving the long years and the painful labors that it needed. But it is not so clear that the rebellious or independent forms of art have the character of discipline to anything like the same degree; and in French art education, as Classicism has been weakened, discipline has been relaxed. Another great virtue in Classicism was its high-minded contempt for the opinion of the uneducated.

In literature, it effectually excluded the vulgar by adopting two languages never used by them, and which could not be mastered without the labor of half a life. In painting it excluded the vulgar, as much as it possibly could, by greatly interpreting, and never imitating, nature, by never illustrating matters of everyday interest, and by a severity of aspect supported by evident erudition; and the consequence of this

bold attitude that Classicism adopted towards persons without culture was that these very persons felt themselves compelled to respect the true students, and no more thought of setting up their crude notions in opposition to culture than an English landowner of the present day thinks of following his own notions of the law in opposition to the advice of counsel. If you set an ignorant person before a page of Greek, or the marble Theseus in the British Museum, he knows and feels that he cannot judge of either of them, which is exactly all that he can be made to know, or required to feel; but, if you give him an English book, or a picture of modern life, he has no hesitation about writing a criticism of one or the other, and selling it for two pounds to some newspaper.

The movement towards more general sympathy which caused the breaking-up of the classical authority was dangerous to art, because it interested the people and made them discuss the matter as if it were within their competence; and the consequence has been that, in these days, though artists have emancipated themselves from a severe and noble tradition, they have fallen under the yoke of a many-headed master, who is in some ways more difficult to serve. The high priests of Classicism did not, it is true, tolerate the slightest divergence from the severity of their law, but the aspirant had the advantage

Joseph-Anton Koch, ▶
1868-1939, Neoclassicism, Austrian, *Swiss Landscape (Berner Oberland)*, 1817. Oil on canvas, 101 x 134 cm. Tiroler Landesmuseum Ferdinandeum, Innsbruck.

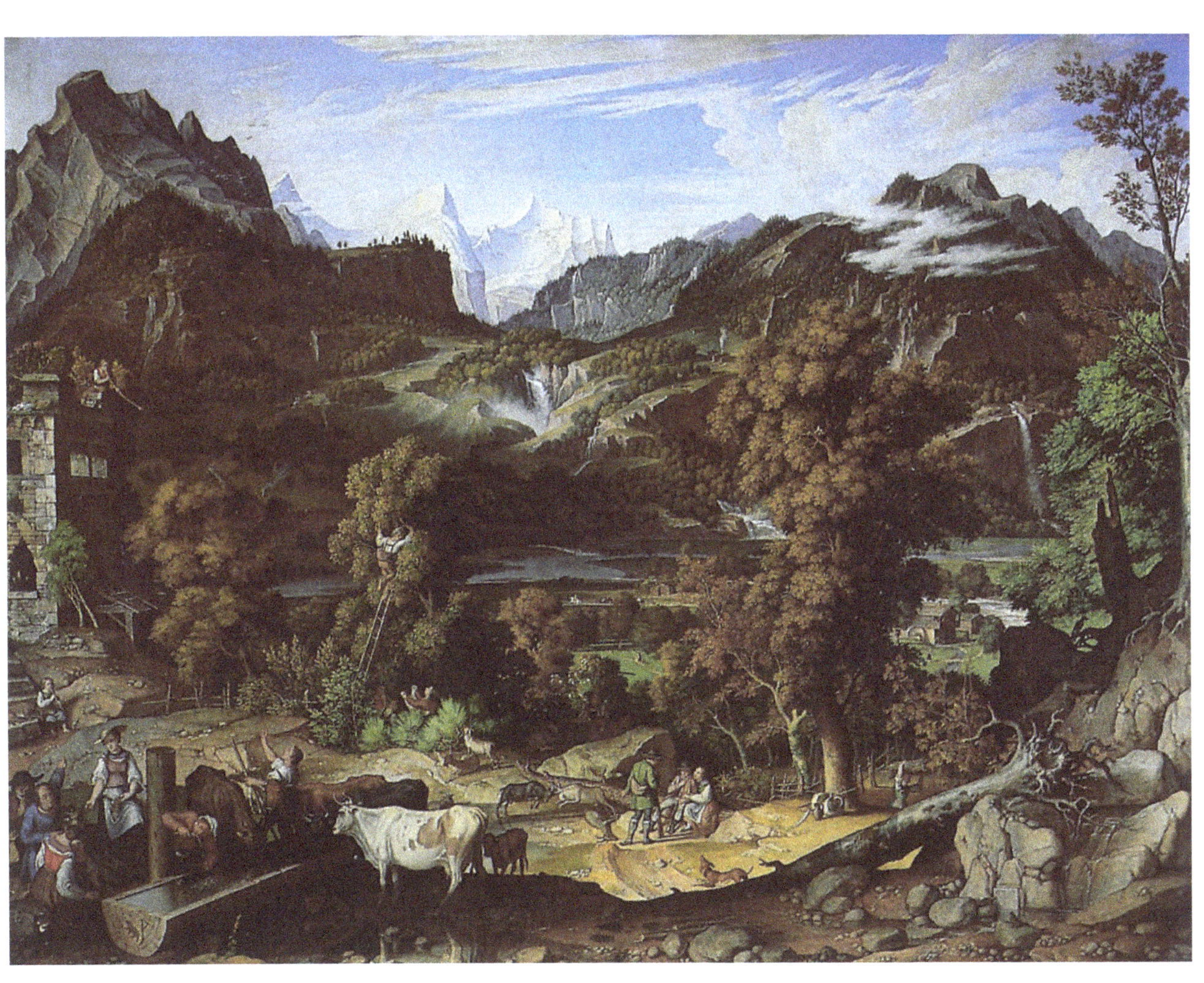

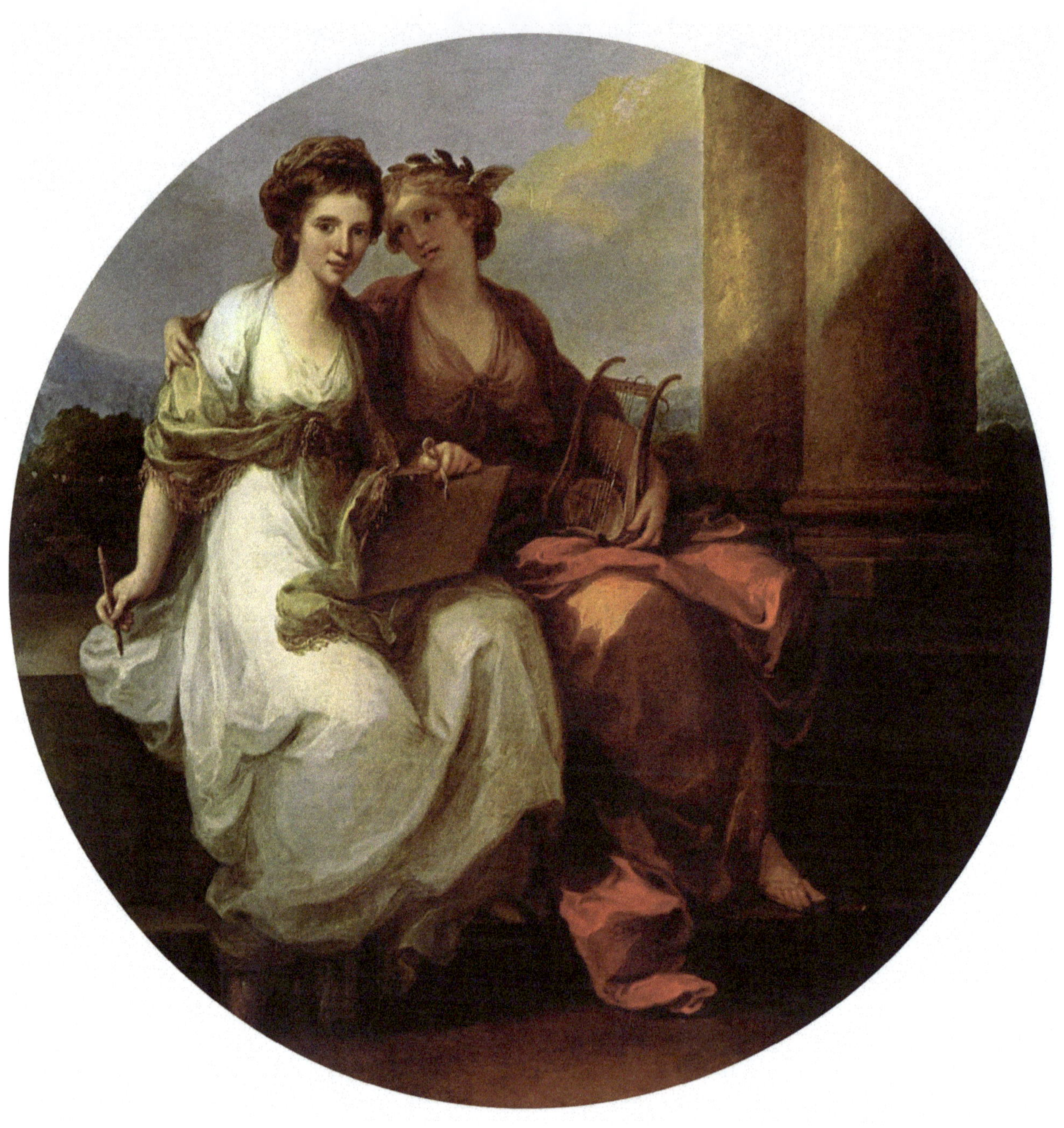

that he could always easily ascertain what was required of him, and knew that his obedience would be rewarded by unfailing encouragement, and his excellence, If he attained it, by honor that was - never withheld. It is not so clear what the modern public wants, or will reward; and many artists labor now in the darkness of a grievous perplexity. Since the public has not yet defined its theory of art, and since all external authority in any degree respectable has now for some time been overthrown, and is not likely to be set up again in our time, I say that the only rule left for an artist to work by is the law of his own sincerest preferences. Modern artists may be broadly divided into two categories: we have those who paint for the market, and those who paint for the pleasure of obeying their own instincts; and the latter are by far the more respectable of the two, and the more likely to do great things. It remains only to be observed that the great danger of painting in obedience to one's own instincts is the possibility of a belief that culture is no longer necessary; whereas even our preferences themselves may be modified by culture, and our faculty of choice improved.

It is impossible to conceive a condition of anarchy more absolute than that which exists at present in the world of art. The Classical doctrine is dead; the Pre-Raphaelite doctrine is dead; the movement of Romanticism was spent long ago, and is now seen to have been a mere temporary enthusiasm, useful as a solvent of Classicism. Even Realism is dead also, or at least gains no new supporters; and the influence of Ruskin, which at one time promised to become dominant in the English school, has ceased even to be perceptible. But although no artistic creed may be consciously received in these days, the work done in them will bear the impress of the time, and be molded by it into something less heterogeneous than the state of apparent anarchy might lead some of us to imagine. If art is not to be allowed to follow much higher ideals than the ideals of society, let us at least hope that it will seldom fall beneath them.

◄ **Angelica Kauffmann**,
1741-1807, Neoclassicism, Swiss, *Allegory of Poetry and Painting,* 1782. Oil on canvas, Tondo, diameter: 61 cm.
Private collection, London.

Jean-Auguste Dominique Ingres, ▶
Odalisque with a Slave, 1839-1840.
Neoclassicism. Oil on canvas,
72.1 x 100.3 cm. Fogg Art Museum,
Harvard University, Cambridge.

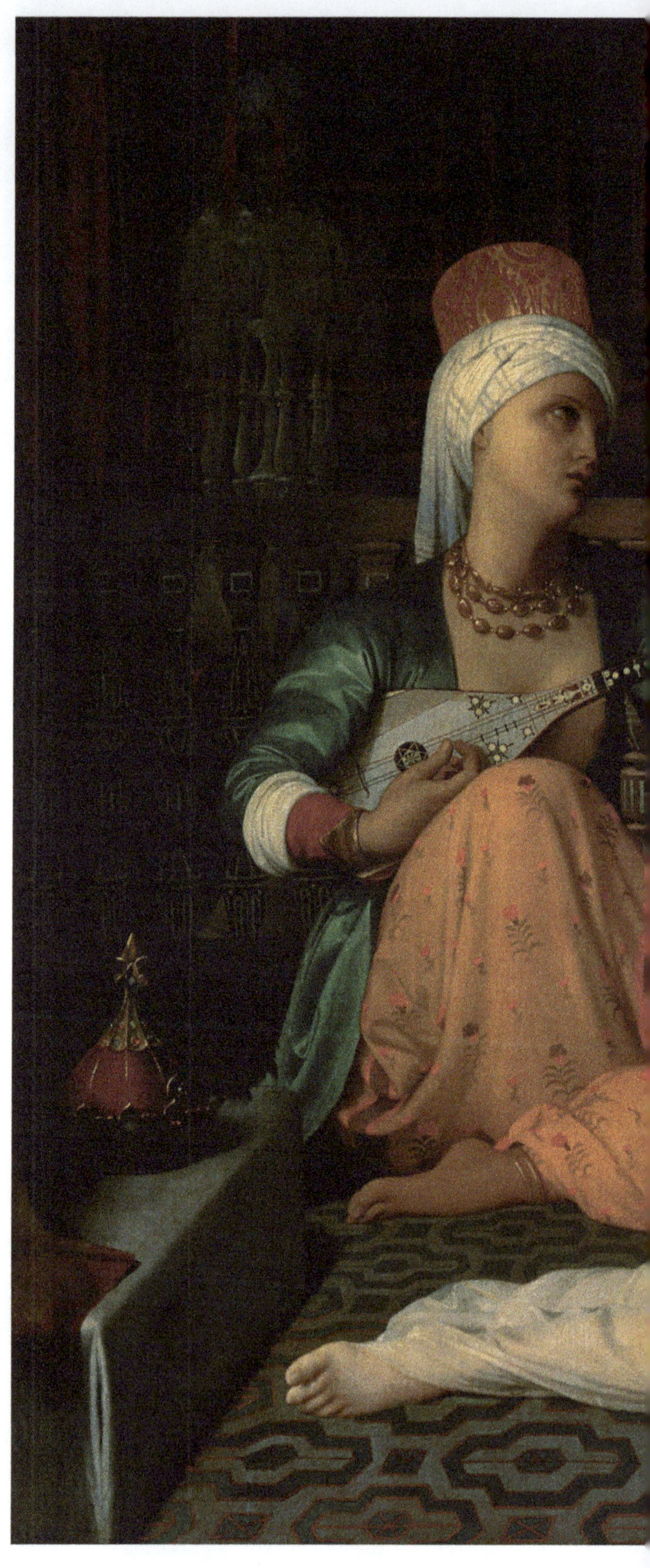

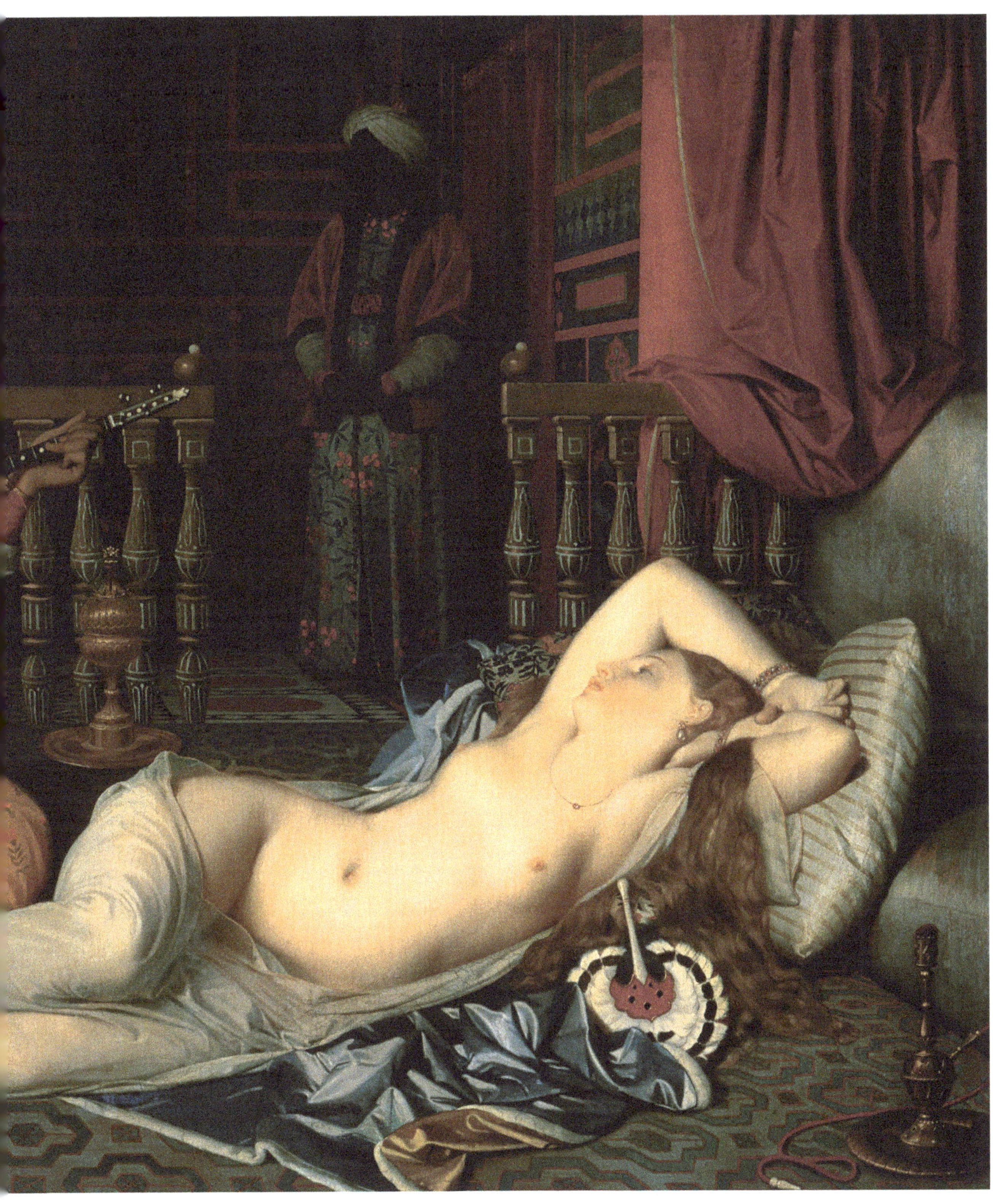

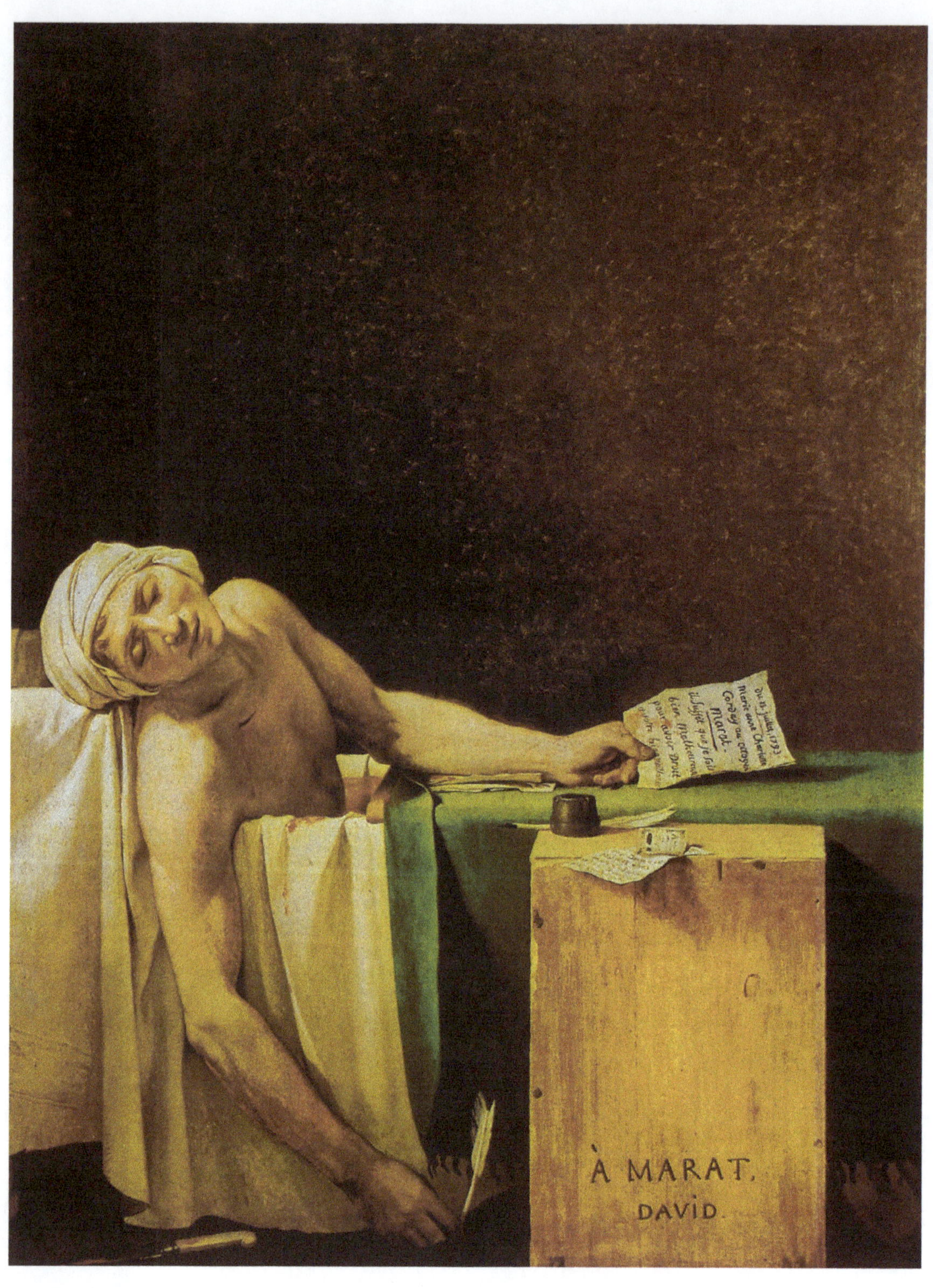

▲ **Jacques-Louis David**, 1748-1825, Neoclassicism, French, *The Death of Marat*, 1793.
Oil on canvas, 162 x 128 cm. Musées Royaux des Beaux-Arts, Brussels.

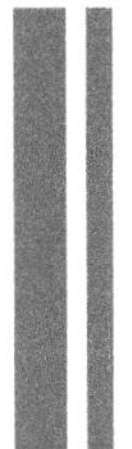# THE ARTISTS

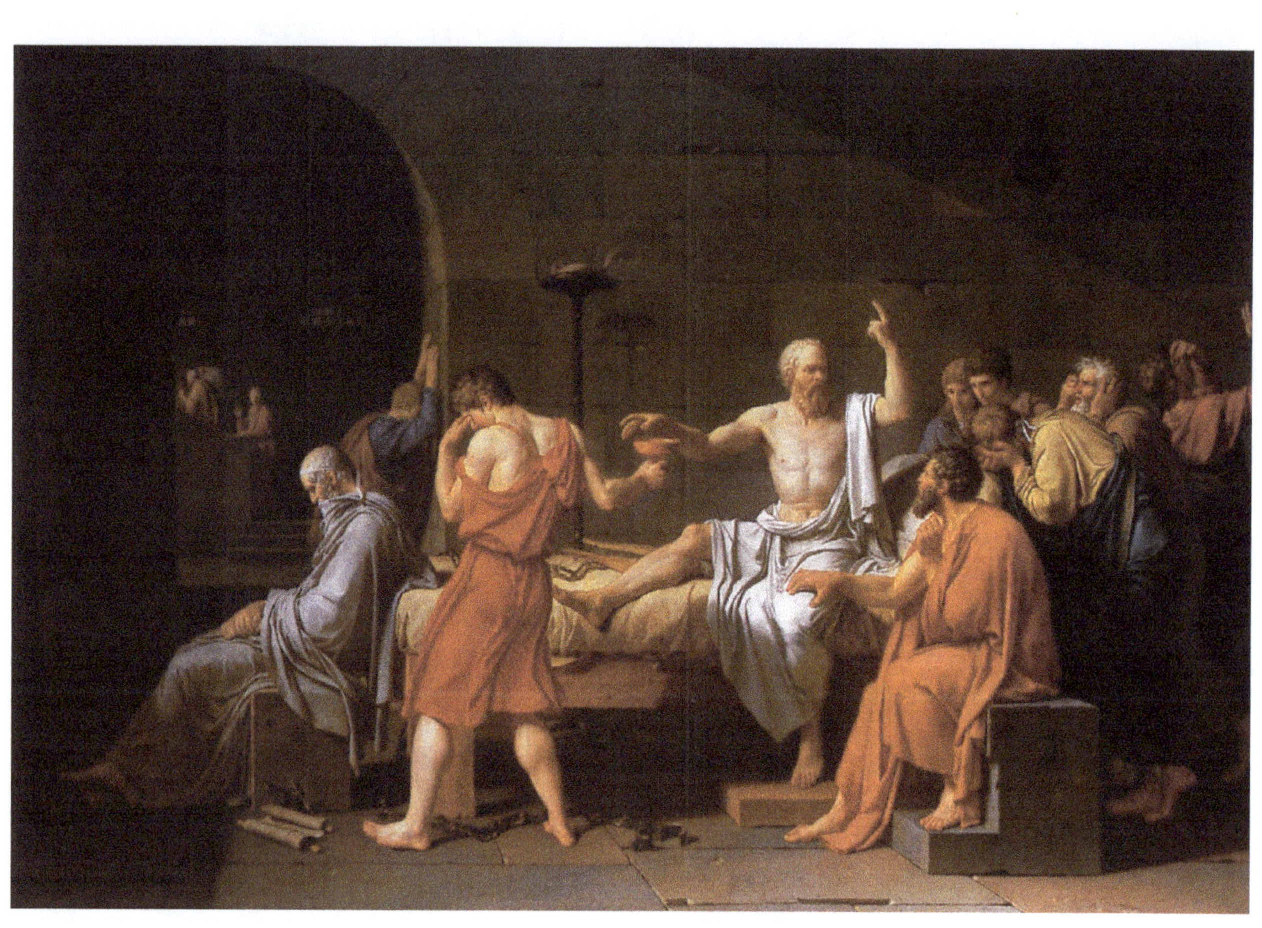

JACQUES-LOUIS DAVID

(1748 PARIS – 1825 BRUSSELS)

acques Louis David, so essentially a French painter, might have taken for his motto the phrase, « Humanism and Reason ». Mankind is always present in his work. He seems to be building monuments with human bodies and, like all worthwhile monuments, those of David are based on sense. The gesture of his Horaces, their arms outstretched, are as full of logic as is that of the Deputies taking the oath of the 'Jeu de Paume'. The composition of his painting of the Sabine Women, not to mention that of the *Coronation of Napoleon*, is founded on a severe geometry of vertical lines cutting horizontal ones at right angles. As a portraitist, David not only gives us the external envelope but the inward character of the sitter. His sincerity, facing his model, is extreme and leads him into the field of the psychologist. Consider that pretty woman of the world, Juliette Récamier; think of that woman of the people called « La Tricoteuse ,» or of M. Pécoul, the prosperous bourgeois, playing unostentatiously with his gold snuffbox. To us, these portraits are as much those of a social caste as of individuals.

No artist was ever more intimately at one with his limes than was Louis David. His canvases, from first to last, bear the stamp of the social class for which they were painted. He sets out to be agreeable and even coquettish when, in the style of Boucher, he embellishes the little establishments supplied by generous tax collectors to their favorites of the Opéra. He becomes severe, depicting phases of the French Revolution when he draws inspiration from the heroes of Greece and Rome. He is profoundly stirred and stirring in painting, for the people, the martyrs of the Revolution, Marat, Lepelletier, de Saint Fargeau, Joseph Bara. His brush knows how to adapt itself to imperial pomp. Whether destined for the brother of Louis XVI, for some rich bourgeois, for the Convention, or for the Emperor, it remains essentially rational and in the tradition of Descartes. Even when he is painting classical subjects with the greatest detachment in the world he never goes beyond verisimilitude and never affronts the rational.

David, the artist, was always manly a Frenchman conscious of his merit, his rights and his duties.

◀ **Jacques-Louis David**,
1748-1825, Neoclassicism, French,
The Death of Socrates, 1787.
Oil on canvas, 129.5 x 196.2 cm.
The Metropolitan Museum of Art, New York.

Elected a deputy, he sat in the Convention. His object there was to prove that art was a national necessity, and the social role of the artist. The speeches which he made in 1792 and 1793 are still valuable today. During a particularly critical period in our history he was not afraid of getting relatively large credits voted for the purchase of paintings by Rubens and Poussin, saying, «it is not right to let these works go out of the country». With brilliant efficiency David organized the 'Muséum Centrai des Arts' which later became the 'Musée du Louvre'. And it was thanks to him that the 'Académie', strangulator of budding talent, was abolished. He allowed all artists, whether French or foreign, to show in the «Salon» and did not consider himself too great a painter to take on lesser kinds of jobs, providing they served a useful purpose. For instance, he consented to design the uniforms of the officials of the Republic. He also took an interest in the theater and in the staging of plays.

When the Convention made him the organizer of the Republican Pageants, David included the people in the parades and gave them, as in classical times, an active role. He handled crowd scenes as they had never before been handled. The pageants of the Republic became demonstrations of a new art of extraordinary breadth. He constructed the 'Festival of the Supreme Being' as he constructed one of his paintings. There is no more whimsy in a work of David than there is in the 'Declaration of the Rights of Man and of the Citizen', but there is the same spirit of precision, of austere confidence. Not a comma is out of place in the one or the other, not a crease in a costume which hasn›t its strict reason for being.

Jacques Louis David was born in Paris in 1748 of well-to-do bourgeois parents who put no hindrance whatever in the way of their son›s vocation. Helped by Boucher›s advice, by lessons with Vien, he won the Prix de Rome in 1774. In Italy, he was impressed by the technique of the Bologna school, so different from that of his French masters. Soon he was seized with a passion for antiquity. The excavations in the ruins of Pompeii and Herculaneum were then subjects of general conversation in the cosmopolitan society of Rome, The German Winkelmann, drew from them the notion of the « Beau Ideal », and the French scholar, Quatremere de Quincy, the theory of the return to the antique. These had a decisive influence on David.

The revolutionary bourgeoisie of Paris welcomed with enthusiasm his painting, *Brutus recevant les corps de ses fils suppliciés* shown at the Salon of 1789, and found in it an example to follow. David, becoming a Jacobin, abolished the Academy of Painting. Elected a deputy to the Convention, he defended art and artists. With his portraits of Marat, of Lepelletier, his art took its place beside the best of French religious painting, the Jacobin expressing his faith as the great unknown painters of the Middle Ages had formerly expressed theirs.

Jacques-Louis David, ▶
1748-1825, Neoclassicism, French,
Oath of the Horatii, 1784.
Oil on canvas, 330 x 425 cm. Musée du Louvre, Paris.

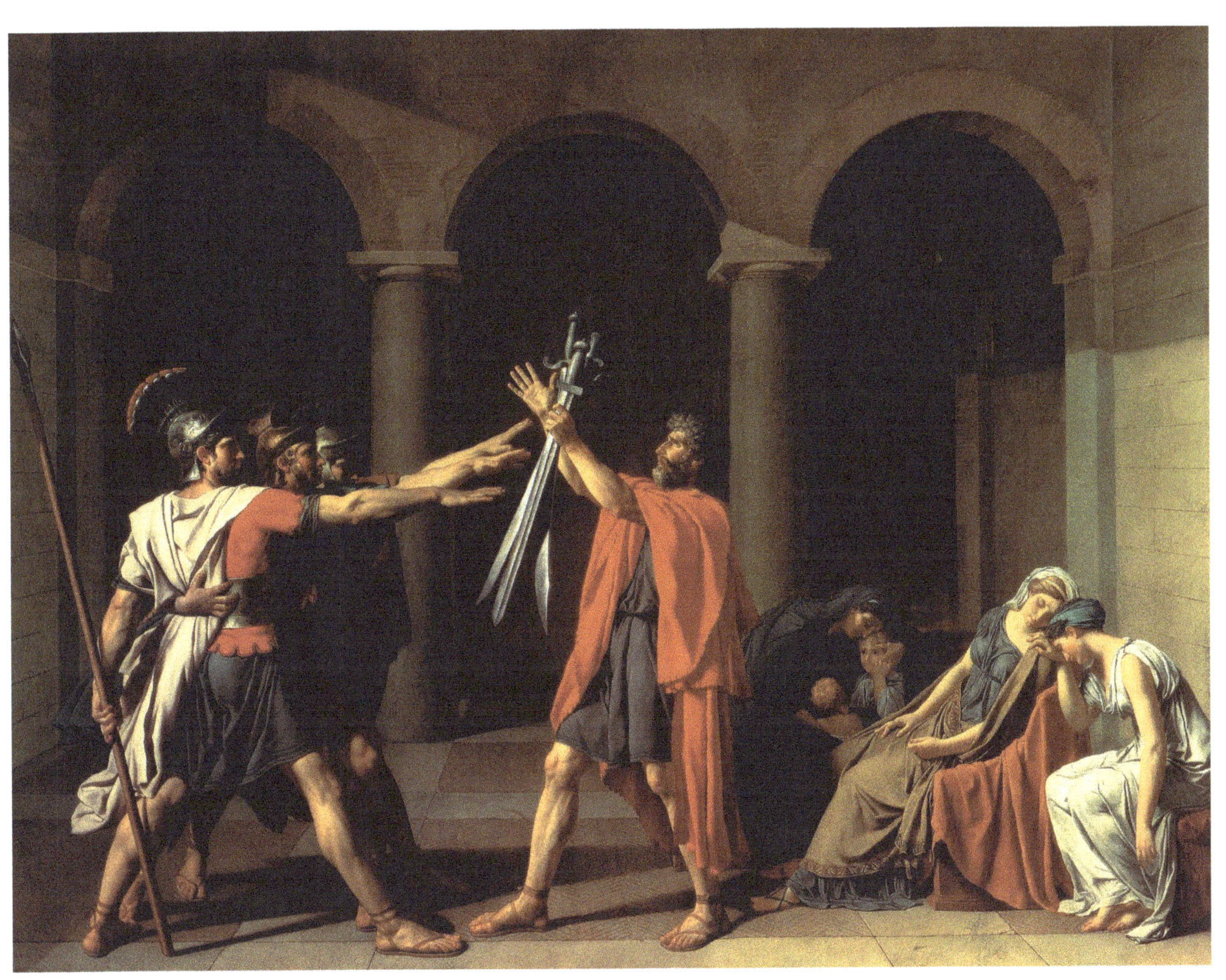

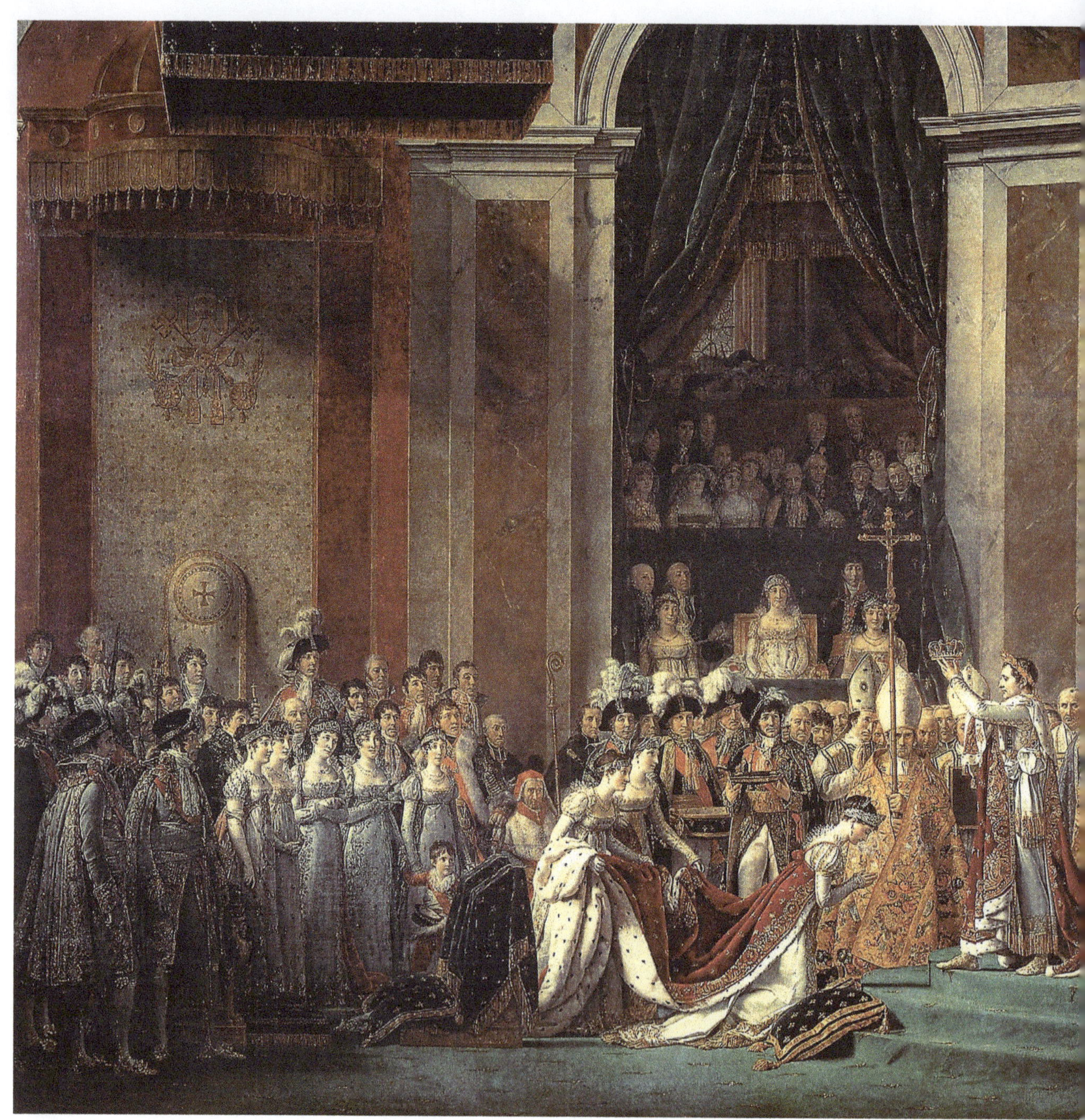

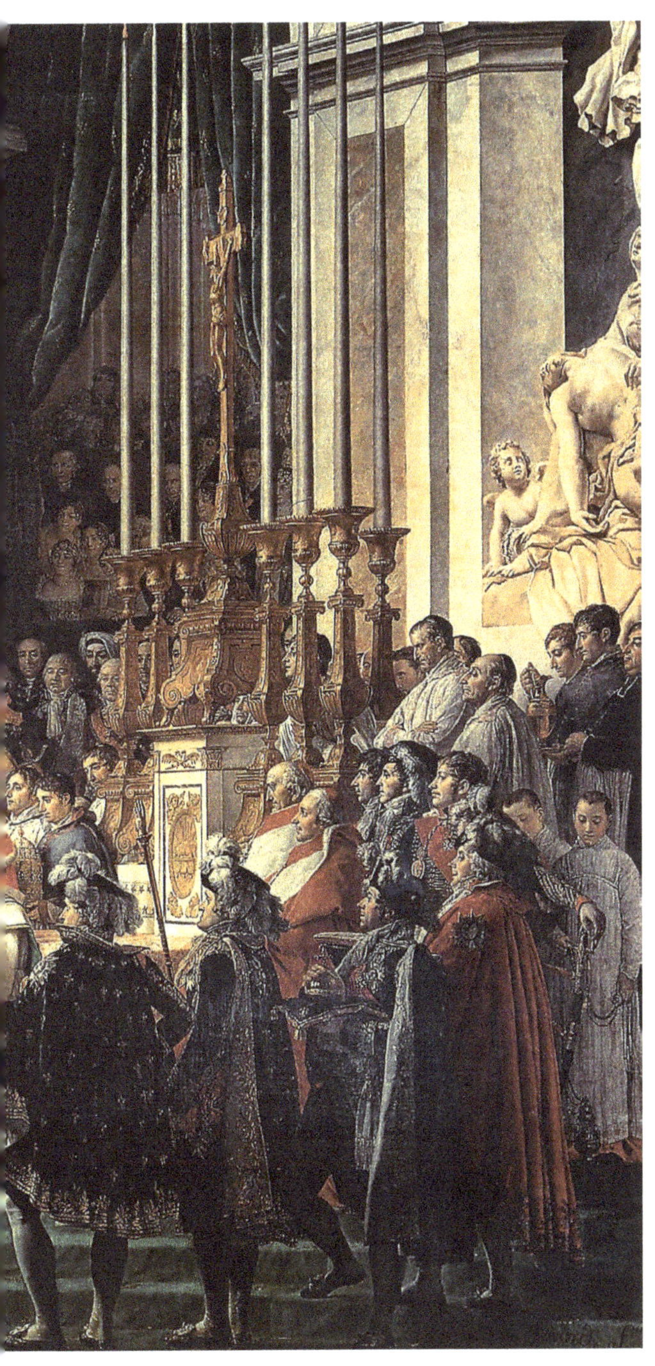

Bonaparte's 'Coup d'Etat' put a violent end to David's republican activities. Soon he was working for the First Consul, then for the Emperor. In painting the *Sacre* (the Coronation of Napoleon as Emperor) he recalls the sumptuousness of a Rubens, that other portrayer of the mighty.

The Restoration sent David into exile, for, as a member of the Convention, they had voted for the execution of Louis XVI. He spent his last years in Brussels, still painting admirable portraits as well as some general subjects. Until the end, he continued teaching, for, throughout his life, his dearest interest was in disciplining young talent. Ingres, his favorite pupil, was to guide other artists, and it is thus, from generation to generation, that classicism comes down to us, for a Picasso to transmit in his turn to the artists of tomorrow.

◀ **Jacques-Louis David,**
1748-1825, Neoclassicism, French,
Consecration of the Emperor Napoleon I and Coronation of the Empress Josephine, 1806-1807.
Oil on canvas, 621 x 979 cm.
Musée du Louvre, Paris.

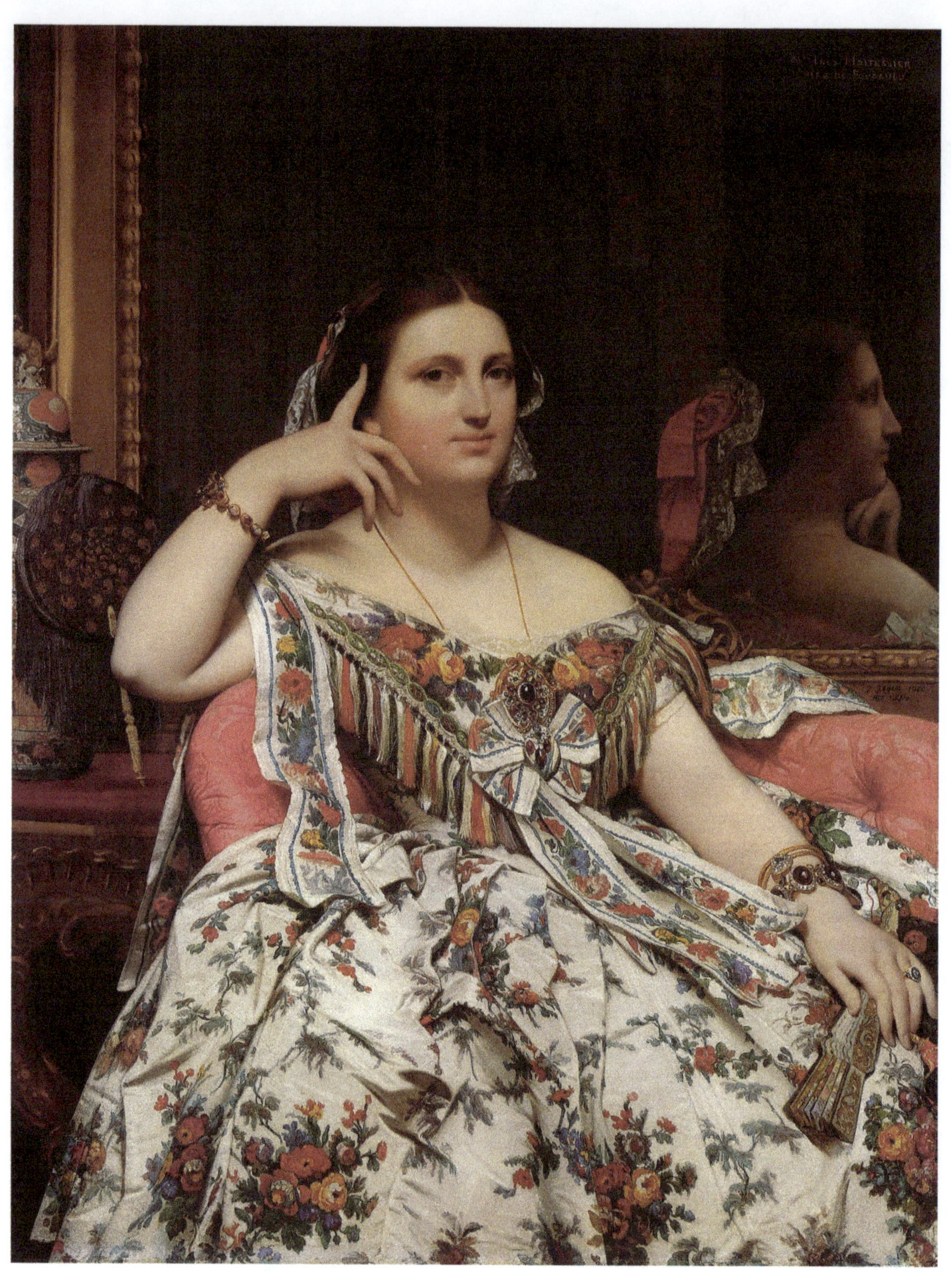

▲ **Jean-Auguste Dominique Ingres,** 1780-1867, Neoclassicism, French, *Mrs Moitessier,* 1856. Oil on canvas, 120 x 92 cm. National Gallery, London.

JEAN–AUGUSTE DOMINIQUE INGRES

(1780 MONTAUBAN – 1867 PARIS)

Ingres at first seemed destined to continue brilliantly the work of his master David both in portrait and historical painting. He won the' Prix de Rome' in 1801. Ingres, however, soon emancipated himself. He was only twenty-five when he painted the Rivière portraits. These show an original talent and a taste for composition not without some mannerism, but the mannerism is full of charm, and the refinement of undulating lines is as far removed as possible from the simple and slightly rough realism which is the strength of David's portraits. His contemporary rivals were not deceived. They attacked his "archaic" and "singular" taste and dubbed him "Gothic" and "Chinese". During the Salon of 1824 however, back from Italy, Ingres was promoted to leader of the Academic style in opposition to the new Romanticism led by Delacroix. In 1834, he was appointed director of the French School in Rome, where he stayed for seven years. Then after his return he was again acclaimed as master of traditional values and finished his days in his home town in southern France.

The biggest contradiction in Ingres' career is his title of 'Guardian of the Classical Rules and Precepts', although we still perceive eccentricity in some of the most beautiful of his works. The back of *La Grande Odalisque* with the oriental setting is a pretext for Ingres to show his virtuosity in the depiction of materials, nacre, and silks. The proportions of the model are wrong, the body is elongated and the face flattened. Ingres got his inspiration from Italian mannerism and, for the arabesques, from the 'School of Fontainebleau'. A pedant, seeing the various exaggerations of form in *The Turkish Bath* would also point to this incomparable draftsman's faults.

But are these not the means by which a great and extremely sensitive artist interprets his passion for the beautiful female form? When he wanted to group a large number of people in a monumental work such as *L'Apothéose d'Homère*, Ingres never attained the ease, the suppleness, the life, or the unity which we admire in the magnificent decorative compositions of Delacroix. On the other hand, he had an impeccable sureness, original taste, a fertile and appropriate invention in the pictures where only two or three figures appear, and even more in those where he illustrates, standing or reclining, a single effigy of the female figure, which was the enchantment and sweet torment of his whole life.

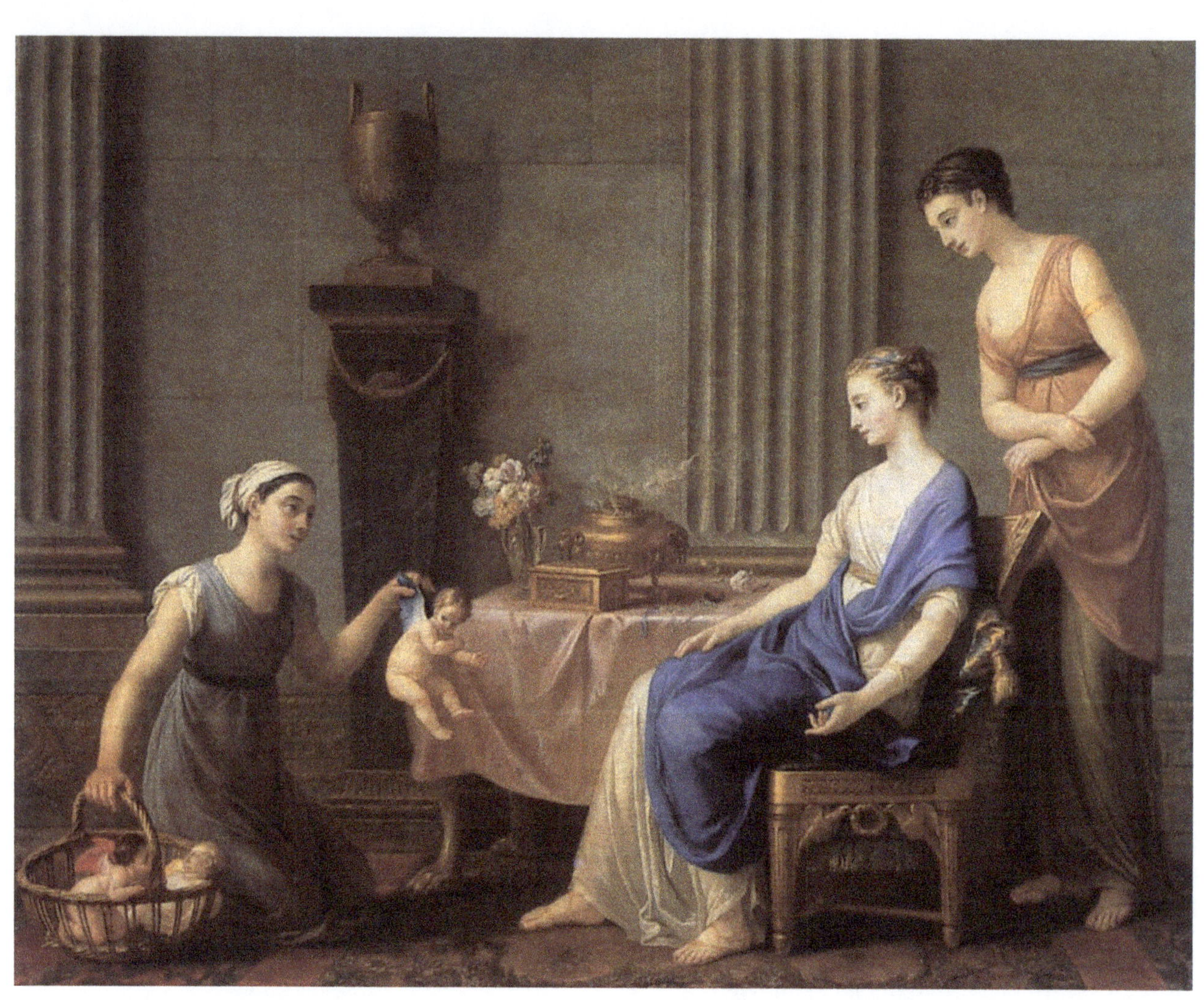

JOSEPH MARIE VIEN

(1716 MONTPELLIER – 1809 PARIS)

Joseph Marie Vien was born on the 18th of June 1716 at Montpellier. Protected by Comte de Caylus, he entered at an early age the studio of Natoire, and obtained the 'Grand Prix' in 1745. He used his time at Rome in applying to the study of nature and the development of his own powers all that he gleaned from the masterpieces around him; but his tendencies were so foreign to the reigning taste that on his return to Paris he owed his admission to the academy for his picture *Daedalus and Icarus* (Louvre) solely to the indignant protests of Boucher.

When in 1776, at the height of his established reputation, he became director of the school of France at Rome but he refused to take David with him amongst his pupils stating that he was too old to teach such a young artist. After his return, five years later, his fortunes were wrecked by the Revolution, but he undauntedly set to work and at the age of eighty (1796) carried off the prize in an open government competition. Bonaparte acknowledged his merit, by making him a senator. He died at Paris on the 27th of March 1809, leaving behind him several brilliant pupils. He was buried in the crypt of the Pantheon.

◀ **Joseph-Marie Vien,**
1716-1809, Neoclassicism, French,
The Seller of Loves, 1763.
Oil on canvas, 98 x 122 cm.
Musée National du Château, Fontainebleau.

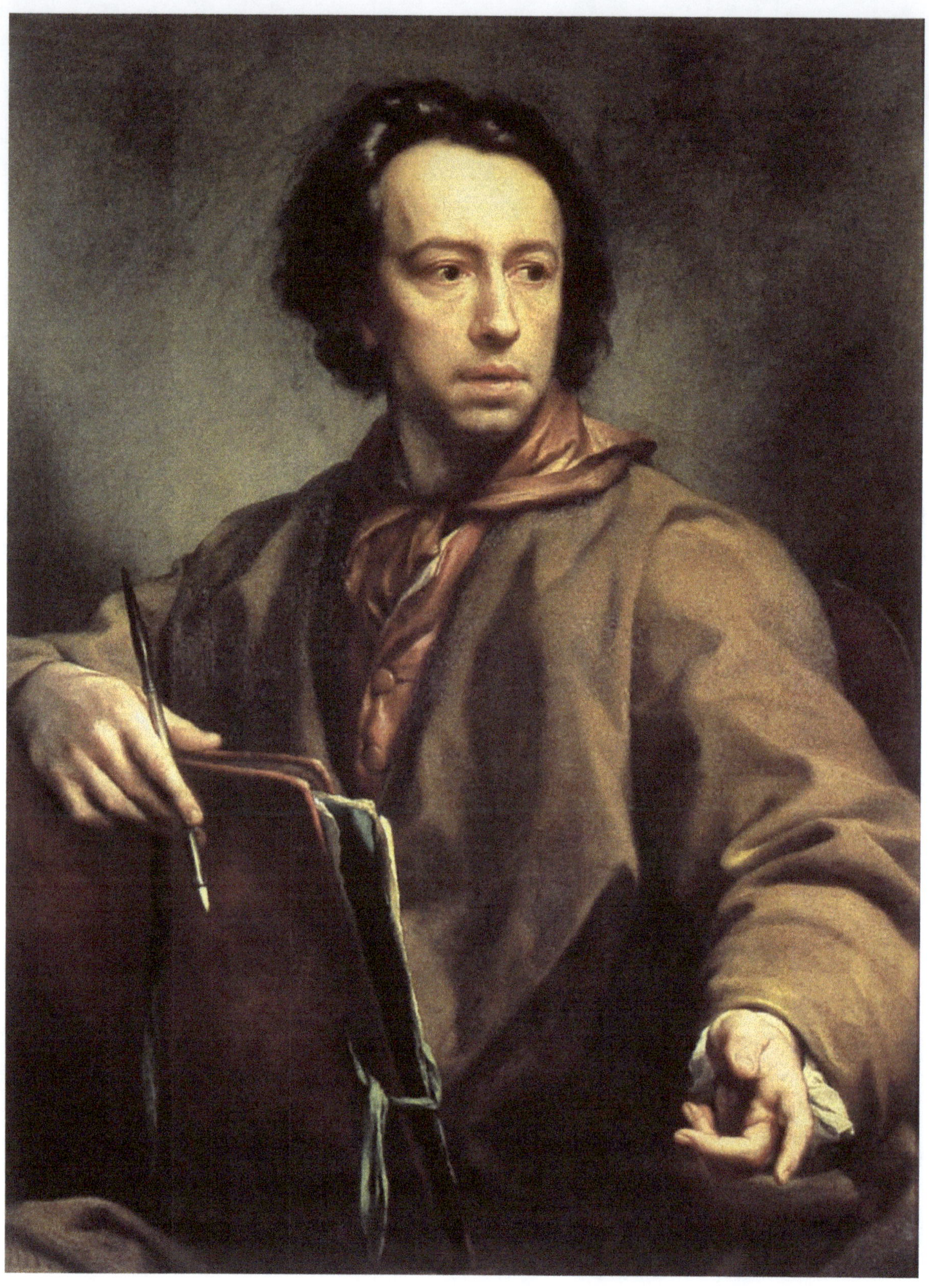

ANTON RAPHAËL MENGS

(1728 AUSSIG – 1779 ROME)

Anton Raphaël Mengs was born in 1728 at Aussig in Bohemia, but his father, Ismael Mengs, a Danish painter, established himself finally at Dresden, whence in 1741 he took his son to Rome. The appointment of Mengs as first painter to the elector of Saxony did not prevent his spending much time in Rome, where he had married in 1748, and abjured the Protestant faith and where he became in 1754 director of the Vatican school of painting, nor did this hinder him on two occasions from obeying the call of Charles III of Spain to Madrid. There Mengs produced some of his best work, and specially the ceiling of the banqueting hall, the subject of which was the *Triumph of Trajan* and the *Temple of Glory.*

After the completion of this work in, 1777, Mengs returned to Rome, and there he died two years later, in poor circumstances, leaving twenty children, seven of whom were pensioned by the king of Spain. Besides numerous paintings in the Madrid Gallery, the *Ascension* at Dresden, *Perseus* and *Andromeda* at St. Petersburg, and the ceiling of the villa Albani must be mentioned among his chief works.

In his writings, in Spanish, Italian and German, Mengs has put forth his eclectic theory of art, which treats of perfection as attainable by a well-schemed combination of diverse excellences – Greek design with the expression of Raphael, the chiaroscuro of Corregio , and the color of Titian. His intimacy with Winckelmann – who constantly wrote at his dictation – has enhanced his historical importance, for he formed no scholars, and the critic must now concur to Goethe's judgment of Mengs: he must deplore that so much learning should have been allied to a total want of initiative and poverty of invention and embodied with a strained and artificial mannerism.

◀ **Anton Raphael Mengs**,
1728-1779, Neoclassicism,
German, *Self-portrait*, c. 1775.
Oil on panel, 97 x 72.6 cm. Galleria degli Uffizi, Florence.

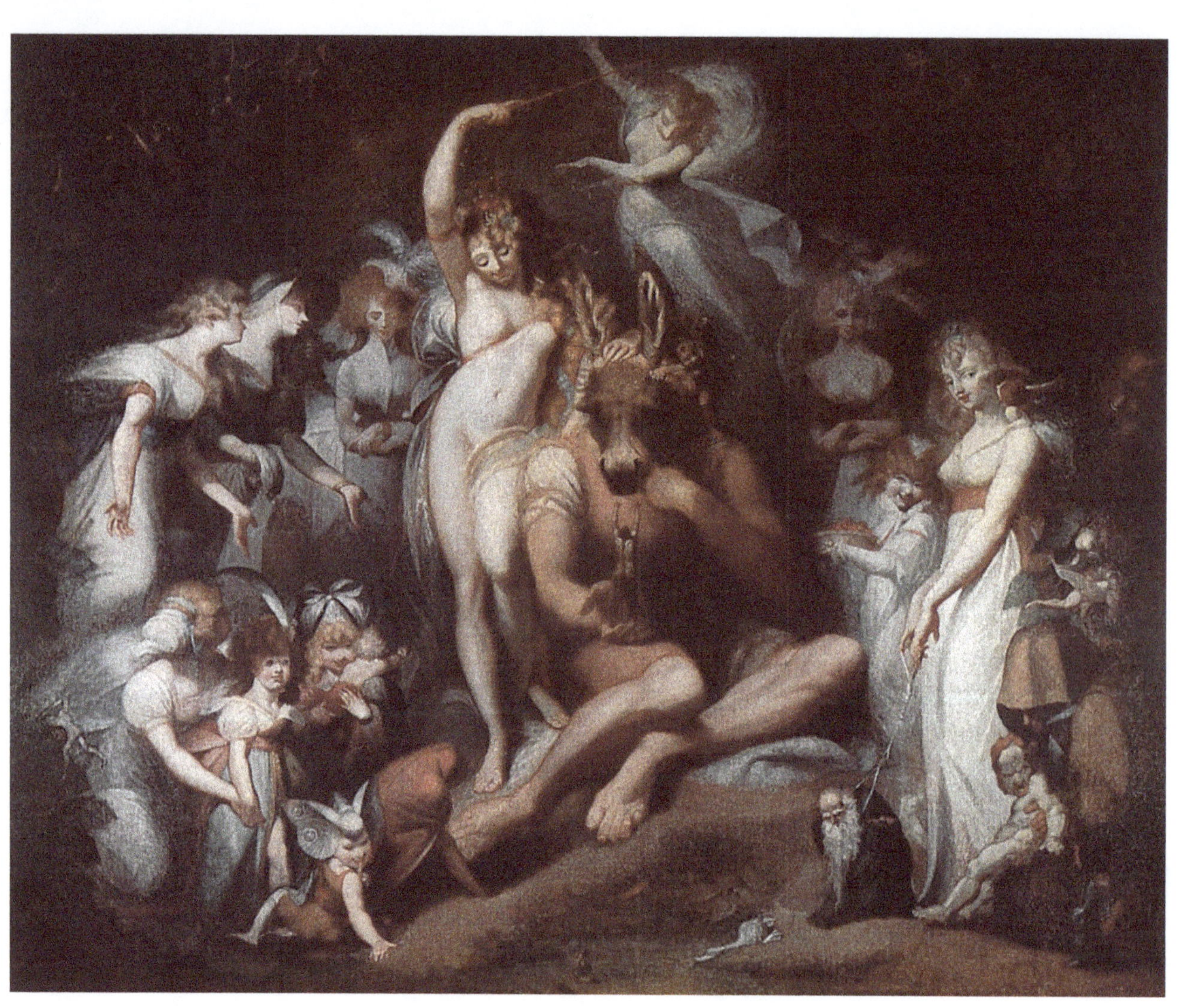

JOHANN HEINRICH FUSELI

(ZÜRICH 1741 – LONDON 1825)

An English painter and writer on art, of German-Swiss family, Fuseli was born in Zürich in Switzerland on the 7th February 1741. His father was John Caspar Füssli, a painter. Fuseli's father intended him for the church, and with this view sent him to the Caroline College of his native town, where he received an excellent classical education.

After taking orders in 1761 Fuseli was obliged to leave his country in consequence of having aided the exposure of an unjust magistrate, whose family was still powerful enough to make its vengeance felt. He first traveled through Germany and then, in 1765, visited England, where he supported himself for some time with writing. He became acquainted with Sir Joshua Reynolds, to whom he showed his drawings. On Sir Joshua's advice, he then devoted himself wholly to art. In 1770, he made an artistic pilgrimage to Italy, where he remained till 1778,

◀ **Johann Heinrich Fuseli**,
1741-1825, Romanticism, Swiss,
Titania and Bottom, 1780-1790.
Oil on canvas, 217 x 275 cm.
Tate Gallery, London.

changing his name from Füssli to Fuseli, as it sounded more Italian. Early in 1779 he returned to England via Zürich. He found a commission awaiting him from an Alderman Boydell, who was then organizing his celebrated Shakespeare gallery. Fuseli painted a number of pieces for this patron.

As a painter, Fuseli was inventive and original and ever aspiring to the highest forms of excellence. His mind was capable of grasping and realizing the loftiest conceptions, which, however, he often spoiled on the canvas by exaggerating the proportions, and throwing his figures into attitudes of fantastic and over-strained contortion. He delighted in the supernatural and idealized his compositions, believing a certain amount of exaggeration necessary in historical painting. "Damn Nature! She always puts me out," was his characteristic exclamation. In this theory, he was confirmed by the study of Michelangelo's works and the marble statues of the Monte Cavallo. But this idea was carried out to excess by him. A striking illustration of this occurs in his picture of *Hamlet and the Ghost*: Hamlet, it has been said, looks as if he would burst his clothes with convulsive cramps in his muscles.

On the other hand, his paintings are never languid or cold. His figures are full of life, earnestness and intense purpose. Like Rubens he excelled in the art of setting his figures in motion. Though the lofty and terrible was his proper sphere, Fuseli had fine perception of the ludicrous. The grotesque humor of his fairy scenes, especially those from *A Midsummer Night's Dream*, is in its way not less remarkable than the poetic power of his more ambitious works. As a colorist Fuseli has but small claims to distinction. He scorned to set a palette as most artists do; he merely dashed his tints recklessly over it. This recklessness may perhaps be explained by the fact that he did not paint in oil until he was twenty-five years of age. Despite these drawbacks he possessed the elements of a great painter.

Fuseli painted more than two hundred pictures, but he exhibited only a minority of them. His first painting to excite particular attention was the *Nightmare*, exhibited in 1782. His sketches or designs number about eight hundred; they have admirable qualities of invention and design, and are frequently superior to his paintings.

Johann Heinrich Fuseli, ▶
1741-1825, Romanticism, Swiss, *The Nightmare*, 1781.
Oil on canvas, 101.6 x 127 cm.
The Detroit Institute of Arts, Detroit.

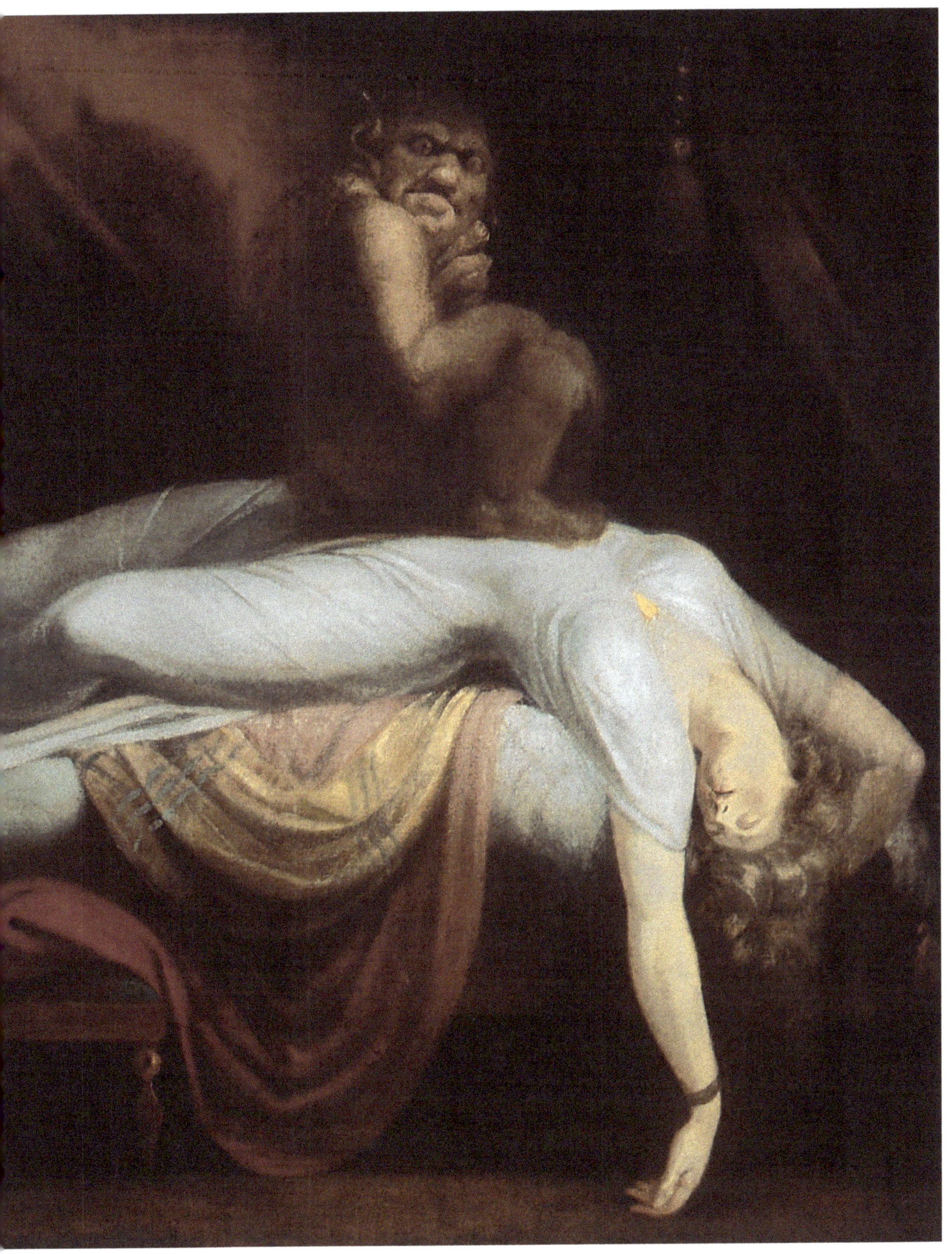

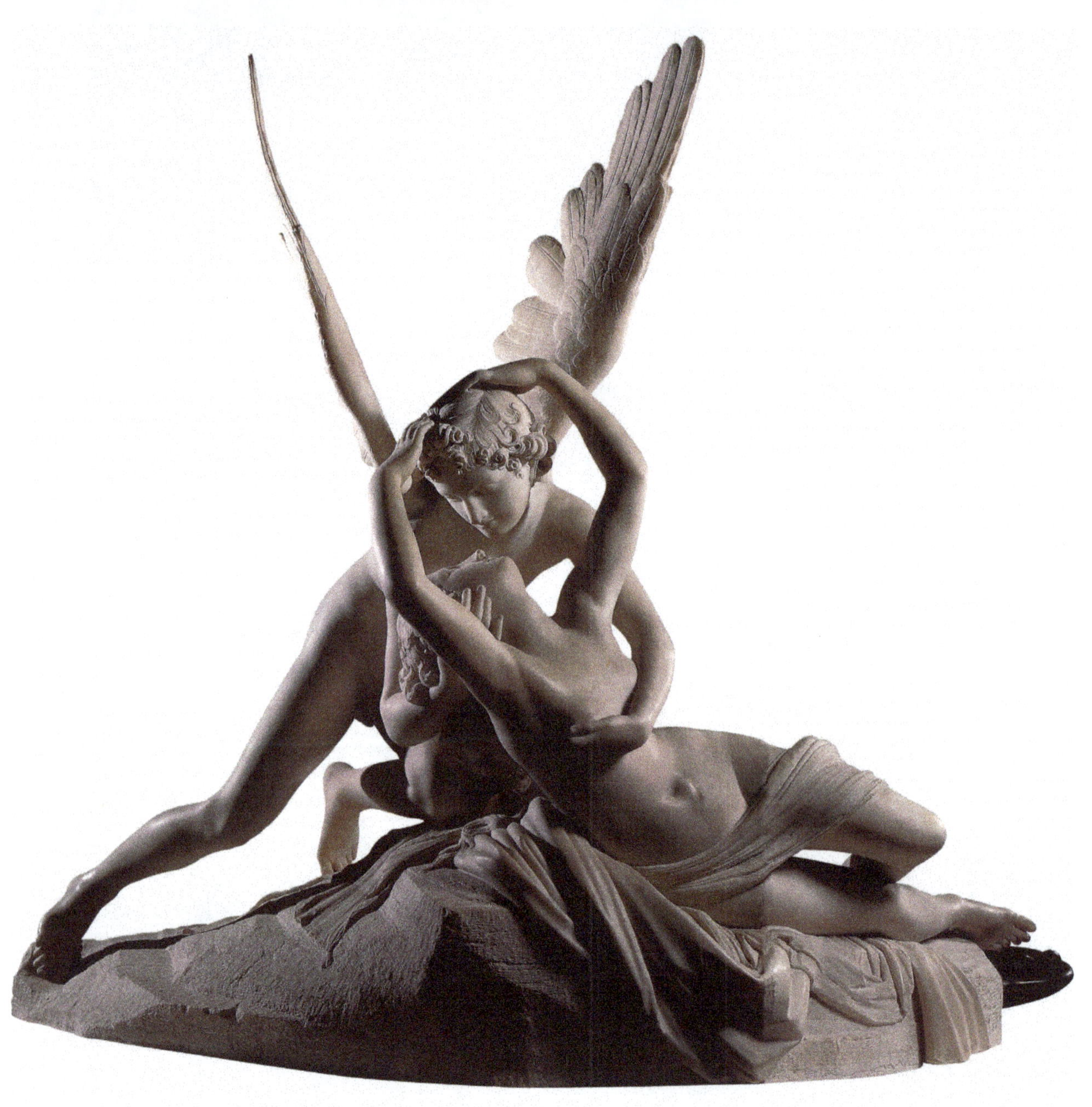

ANTONIO CANOVA

(1757, POSSAGNO – 1822, VENICE)

talian sculptor Antonio Canova was the grandson of a talented stonemason and spent his early life with him modeling in clay. His talent was obvious; the influential Senator Falieri noticed the young boy and had him placed with the sculptor Torretto, to learn his art. At the age of sixteen, he created his first work, *Eurydice*, followed by *Orpheus*, *Daedalus and Icarus*. Canova went to Rome in 1780, where he was strongly influenced by classical Antiquity. During this time, he modeled a masterpiece called *Theseus and the Minotaur* which is today in Vienna. He produced many other admirable works in Rome, including *Psyche Awakened by Eros* in the Louvre, and *Creugas and Damoxenus* in the Vatican Gallery.

He was admired by Napoleon from whom he received an important commission to execute a colossal statue of him. He became the imperial sculptor and portraitist of Napoleon's mother, Marie-Louise, Pauline Bonaparte and many other members of the court. In Vienna, he was charged with the creation of a monument for Maria Christina, the Archduchess. His most famous portrait is probably the *Bust of Pius VII*, created in 1807. Promoted by the Pope, given the title of Marquis of Ischia, Canova made a huge statue named *Religion*. Many other commissions followed, among which feature famous masterpieces such as *Infant St John*, *The Recumbent Magdalena*, a statue of Washington and his *Pietà*. Other important commissions include the tombs of two popes, Clement XIII and Clement XIV. Buried in Possagno, where he was born sixty-five years earlier, Canova is considered the artist who defined classical, elegant sculpture and was of primary importance in the development of the neoclassical style.

◀ **Antonio Canova**,
Psyche Awakened by Eros, 1787-1793. Neoclassicism.
Marble, 55 x 68 x 101 cm.
Musée du Louvre, Paris.

LIST OF ILLUSTRATIONS

ART HISTORY COLLECTION

Abstract Art	Naive Art
Art Deco	Neoclassicism
Art Nouveau	Persian Art
Baroque	Post-Impressionism
Byzantine Art	Realism
Chinese Art	Renaissance
Cubism	Pre-Raphaelites
Dada	Rococo
Early Italian Art	Roman Art
Egypt Art	Romanesque Art
Expressionism	Romanticism
Gothic Art	Surrealism
Greek Art	Symbolism
Impressionism	The Fauves
Indian Art	The Viennese Secession